Hooper's Pasture

Hooper's Pasture

from Maine *to* Vermont

John S. Hooper

Illustrated by Jeff Danziger

The New England Press
Shelburne, Vermont

The New England Press, Inc.
P.O. Box 525
Shelburne, Vermont 05482

Library of Congress Catalog Card Number: 82-81066
ISBN 0-933050-12-7

The author and the publisher wish to acknowledge that the essays in this book first appeared as weekly columns in the following newspapers: the Portland *Press Herald* and the Waterville *Morning Sentinel* in Maine and the *Brattleboro Reformer,* the *Sunday Times Argus,* and the *Sunday Rutland Herald* in Vermont.

PRINTED IN THE UNITED STATES OF AMERICA

Preface

The writing in this book is, in essence, two-faced. I am a Maine-iac born and a Vermonter retired. In the 75 years of my living days, up to this point, my loyalty and experiences have been divided mostly between these two states.

This is not an autobiography, however. Perish the thought. But it is an account of living moments, gleaned from a lifetime, while looking back and around during my more recent sojourn in the confines of my retirement pasture.

I am by nature and training a reporter, and this book is a report of things that happened—not only to me but to my immediate family, to my parents and relatives, to people I have known. Let's say, as a long-time newspaperman, this is my own personal journal, with a dateline rather late in life, and offering you a particular kind of news from two states that have more in common than just the fact that I happened to live in them.

The title of this correspondent's reporting merely indicates the location of his present news desk—"Hooper's Pasture."

Contents

Hooper's Pasture

Nibbling on the Years

As a man grows older, along with his homestead and the trees around it, he thinks less in terms of his birthdays than in well-defined periods in his life. You can't actually see a tree grow, but you can see, every few years, that the pines you and the boy put out a few years back are suddenly taller than your head. And when you look back thirty years to the open pasture above the barn, you wonder how all that pasture became covered with twenty-foot hemlocks so quickly.

That's how a countryman counts the years of his life, not by birthdays. There were the years of the ponies, when with the youngsters he was reliving his own childhood affection for his Shetland stallion. It didn't occur to him that the ponies were more for himself than for the children, or that he probably enjoyed cleaning them out more than they did. But it's the baseball enthusiast who wants to make sure that his children get the pleasure of Little League, or the ardent fisherman who patiently totes his small son out to the brook the father fished as a child.

This is the period of getting used to the idea of living with children, the period when the father unconsciously is merging his own childhood memories with his hopes and aspirations for the new family and another generation.

There is the longer period when the rural home and acres are not only filled with the family activities, cut out to fit the four seasons and altered through the years to fit changing interests, but the home acres are a place to move from and back to as the youngsters' interests expand. These constitute most of the school years.

No single parental birthday stands out in those years. In retrospect, they are a period in which the parent must have grown older. The children certainly did. But he passed his fortieth and even his fiftieth birthday without their making much of a ripple on his awareness of time's passing. Grudgingly, he admitted to a few more aches and pains, but he passed those off onto a rainier spring or unseasonal cold spells. What's a birthday, anyhow? Just another ring in the growing tree.

The average countryman is on all kinds of mailing lists. He gets printed sales pitches by the dozen every day. He receives cards from his insurance agent each birthday, expressing hope that he will "have lots more of them," but not expressing the obvious pleasure that the old cuss is still alive and paying premiums. He hears too frequently from the Internal Revenue Service that another year is about to come to a close. But only once, only once, does he get a particular kind of government letter.

It said, "We here at your Social Security District Office are aware that you are about to reach your sixty-fifth birthday. We are pleased to inform you are now eligible for Medicare."

Well, now, that was a birthday to take notice of. Still, to a countryman surrounded by ever-changing beauty and abundance of growing things, it merely marked the beginning of another period in life.

This other period includes more birthdays, as regular as hands on the clock. But it is a period of new experiences because it includes one final factor, the beginning of retirement.

First, he fights it by setting up a small advertising business that he operates for about three years, maintaining some of the day-to-day routine he had left at the newspaper. After five years of this delay in actual retirement, he decides to close this small business.

The countryman had finally been put out to pasture. This is a period of slower pace, of different routine, of new experiences.

From the pasture, one view is distant, looking out over a lifetime. He is not concerned with counting the years, but with nibbling on them here and there.

And there is a closer view, the day-to-day looking at the things he wants to do, or needs to do, and making his selection.

No routine limits this period. It has its long view and short view—one to reminisce about, one to anticipate and indulge in. It is the freest period for selection, no matter which direction he looks.

It is like planting trees again, only the roots of these are within him.

Telephones Had a Personality

THE VOICELESS DIAL telephone is convenient and efficient—if you can remember the digits long enough. And it still sometimes has a voice of its own when you have slipped up on those digits. A nasal, tinny voice on tape suddenly snaps you out of your anticipated conversation with: "The number you are calling is not in service. Will you please hang up and dial again?" So you look up the number again and you simply hadn't put your finger in the right slot. You dial again, having almost forgotten what you had in mind when the whole process started. This is known as the "computer syndrome," and I haven't become used to it yet.

What I mean is that for so many years I did not have to deal with the American Telephone & Telegraph mechanized service every time I took the telephone off the hook but was directly involved with a person called a telephone operator and a person whom in most cases I knew personally. I am not belittling the current efficiency of this form of communication; I am simply still aware of what it has replaced.

Until the dial moved in and the local switchboard was moved out, one of the most useful and necessary individuals, especially in a small community, was the local telephone operator. She not only was often a helping hand in the process of making a phone call, but quite as often was a source of information that no computer can provide.

This was especially important in the case of newspaper reporters. We used to ask them the darndest questions about something we needed to know in Newfane, Wardsboro, or even Bellows Falls, and get a decent answer. "Is John Smith still in town or has he already gone to Florida? I don't seem to get an answer for the past several days." The information is that he has already gone to Florida.

The telephone was probably the most important device invented to turn isolated homes into a community. One already had neighbors to talk with over the back fence or at the general store. Suddenly, one had a whole community to talk with, including the telephone operator.

I am taking here an experience I had in Maine, because I am sure the same thing was happening all over Vermont and around the country at the same time some sixty years ago.

At about the age of ten or twelve I was a privileged observer of the inside of the Deer Isle, Maine, telephone office. The same sort of office existed in just about every town in New England, only this one was in a building whose rear end was supported by posts driven into the beach to keep it above high water. Vermont offices were located on drier soil and often almost obscured by the overhanging branches of maple trees, or even elms.

My chance to see an early switchboard at work arose because it was operated by my cousin, Bea Knowlton. And this is the sort of thing that went on in that little room:

"Just a minute, Alice," I heard the operator say, "I have to get George Simpson through to Ellsworth and then I'll come back to you." Then, a minute or two later, "Now, Alice, what was it you wanted? Whether the Benedicts have opened there summer home? Not yet. But they are expected around July 15. Hello, hello, operator. . . ."

No matter how important Uncle Perce's newspaper was, it only came out once a week. Cousin Bea, or her assistant, was available twenty-four hours a day. A community was a community in those days, with the crucial link being the telephone operator. She had a board in front of her with what seemed like hundreds of holes. Her hands would flit all over the board, pushing in or pulling out pegs on the ends of innumerable wires. And all the time she was talking.

"Hi! Edie!" Bea would say. "You want to reach Fred? Better wait a while, because I just saw him walk across the street to the Post Office. By the way, you going to the supper down at Green's Landing? Good. I'll see you there."

With the sixteen hands an operator seemed to have, she would continue in this way for hours. If Cousin Carl dropped by — and somehow he seemed to know just about when that time should be — Bea would jump down from her high stool and take a short break, perhaps getting a cup of coffee before again mounting the stool Carl had temporarily taken over. He was pretty good at it, too, only sometimes he would tell a particular friend a joke or two, which perhaps should not have gone out over a telephone switchboard. There were some eight-party lines!

If, as I suppose, there are still some telephone operators in some rural areas, my hat is off to them. And I am glad to have this opportunity to salute their thousands of predecessors.

Now, what was that number I was just about to dial?

Two in a Pasture

ONE DAY RECENTLY I was walking through another pasture, some distance from the one that rises above my own rural house. I was pushing my way through juniper bushes, as seems to be usual these days in many of Vermont's formerly open areas, when I came face to face with a chestnut-colored quarter horse. He was a beautiful example of his breed, and from the roughness of his body hair I could see that he had not been groomed for some time but simply put out to pasture to graze until somebody might decide to take him back to the barn and shape him up for riding again.

We said a sort of quiet hello, and he came to where I was standing. I sat down and looked out with him at the view from his particular pasture.

"Nice view," I said. He nodded, presumably in agreement.

I sat there thinking about this obviously very useful animal simply wandering about a hillside pasture, to no apparent purpose.

It then occurred to me that he really was doing quite a lot, in his own way and quite independently. With plenty of exercise, he was keeping in good health. With a hill to look from, he was far more free than if pent-up in a barn stall. And he exuded contentment.

Sitting there with the horse—we were the only occupants of his hill—I found my thoughts wandering back to the companionship a pony had given me in my newsboy days, back to the delightful stable smells of my uncle's livery stable in those same boyhood days—with only the quiet munching of hay at feeding time and an occasional hoof stamped on the stable floor to shake of a horsefly. In that reverie I could also see the shiny carriages and wagons lined up in the long shed, awaiting the next day's business when the traveling salesmen—*drummers* they were called—would arrive to hire a horse and carriage for making their calls around town and to the nearby towns.

I could see also, in a not-so-distant past, the old pacing mare and sulky I once had here on Sunset Lake Road, and the joy of being alone with her when the entire road was of dirt and over which she could still set a reasonably fast pace, whisking the day's labors at the newspaper office from my mind as my hands concentrated not on a typewriter communicating with unseen readers but on the pair of reins with which I was communicating solely with her.

The mind's view from that hill, sitting with the horse who no longer seemed a stranger, included my own quarter horse in a more recent past and the days of riding over the backroads that abound in this section of Vermont—seldom meeting a car, in contrast to the abundance of them on the backroads at present.

For some of us who grew up in the days when the horse was king, and for many people nowadays—especially young people who in increasing numbers have discovered that horses provide a warm kind of companionship—there is a sort of wordless communication between horse and human that is different from that between humans and smaller animals that become pets. A horse is not a pet but an animal friend whose size and potential for exerting its own will require understanding and respect.

I withdrew from the long view back and let my eyes settle on the immediate view my new-found friend on the hill and I were sharing. In the distance was a low range of New Hampshire mountains. Between us and them was the Connecticut River. Along its banks were flat fields on which many times of the year there is considerable farm activity.

I stood up and rubbed my hand along the horse's back. I instinctively rubbed my face along the side of his head.

"We've just shared something, my friend," I thought. "We have shared the beautiful view spread out before us. We have shared the knowledge that each of us has had an active life, perhaps at times being driven against our will. But we have also just shared the sense of being alive, being friendly, and being contented on a Vermont hillside under a warm sun and with mountains and a river that will long survive both of us. Each of us still has work to do, but not as relentlessly as in the past."

Old-Fashioned Remedies

As I WAS SAYING to my 102-year-old mother the other day, "Mom, times have changed." Both our hearing aids were working well, and we were having a good conversation over the phone, being able to go far beyond the "How's the weather?" exchange.

I had told her that I had a slight cold.

"You don't happen to have some Musterole around, do you?" she asked. "Rub some on your chest, if you do."

I told her that it had been a long time since I had seen Musterole in the medicine closet. Then I asked her what was in that bag she used to hang around my neck when I was very young, something I wore all winter to prevent colds.

"That was pieces of camphor in a bag made of cotton cloth

that I sewed and put a string through. It seemed to do the trick. You didn't have many colds, but how it did smell," she said.

I suggested that what did the trick might have been the smell, sort of something oozing up into the nose that you buy in sprays and drops these days. This reminded me of camphorated oil and flannel cloth. It even reminded me of mustard plasters, some kind of paste made with powdered mustard and spread on a cloth and applied to the skin of the chest that seemed to be the recipient of all the early medical nostrums.

"You didn't have any mustard plasters," she said. "Those were back in my own childhood." I didn't dispute her, but mustard plasters remain vivid.

I mentioned goose grease, and again got a negative response. I can still smell it. In fact, I wonder what the smells were like in the one-room school whose pupils my mother taught some eighty-five years ago—especially in winter with a hot woodstove in the middle of a small room packed with children from kindergarten to the eighth grade.

Anyhow, it gave me the opportunity to ask what were some of the medicines she had nearly a hundred years ago.

"My father was a great believer in Epsom salts," she said. "Each of us children had to take a small swallow every morning. It seemed to do us good, although I can't say that I enjoyed it." I said that I hoped they weren't big swallows and she replied, "No, they were just sips."

"There's one thing we all did when I was young," she said. "It was common to wear a nutmeg, pierced to let a string through, hung around the neck."

"What in the world was that for?" I asked.

"It prevented boils," she said, with a chuckle showing that she didn't think much of it. Its purpose, however, indicates that there were vitamin deficiencies or diet inadequacies that in the isolated towns of New England produced problems that have long since been removed. Having seen a picture of my mother at the age of sixteen, a beautiful young woman, it is hard to realize that under that buxom bodice was a nutmeg hung on a string.

"We did the best with what we had," she said. It certainly didn't do her any harm.

I think of these old medicines and wonder what the consumer reporters would have been saying about such things, if they had existed and were as detailed in the daily analysis of some medicine or product or habit as they are in the prime-time news shows of today. I can just hear them: "Such-and-such a test has found that nutmegs worn around the neck are dangerous to one's health."

One thing that is not exactly a medicine, but that was invented more than 100 years ago by a Maine doctor as a "nerve food," remains today one of my favorite drinks. Moxie long ago lost its status as a health food—although there always were several bottles out in the icebox in my childhood days. It was considered a "tonic." Its fame in its early days contributed to the saying—about a person who had lots of pep, personality, and vigor—"That chap has plenty of moxie."

Forgetting that, I am one of the oddballs who like it just for its taste. A UPI story recently stated that it is being successfully promoted for just that—even though its taste is bittersweet.

The new promotion of this soft drink says, "You know, Moxie goes well with rum and vodka, too." Why spoil a good drink, when you don't have to? It's like spoiling orange juice with castor oil, which earlier parents thought was a good way to cover the taste of what they believed you needed.

Moxie may no longer be a tonic kept in the icebox on the back porch, but some of us still like it when we can find it— cold and refreshingly bittersweet. Come to think of it, perhaps I should send a bottle to my mother. It might help her reach a ripe old age.

12

Gathering the News

My Uncle Perce, on his isolated Deer Isle, Maine, met the 20th century face to face. He was the nosiest man on this coastal island, and he had to be to survive his two separate, but interlocked, careers.

He was the owner and editor of the *Deer Isle Messenger,* published every Thursday. He was also first selectman of Deer Isle, a position he clung to for a number of years by carefully cultivating his politics while, equally carefully, avoiding controversy in his editorials. He reported the meetings of the selectmen in detail and thus put the burden of unpopular increase in the cost of local government on the board rather than on himself as editor of the island's only newspaper, which needed all the good will (and subscriptions) it could get — as well as advertisers.

To keep his newspaper solvent, with its ancient handpress and typecase, he had to know at least something about everything his subscribers wanted to read about, which was primarily about what everybody else on the island (linked to the mainland by ferry) had been doing during the previous week. They expected Uncle Perce's *Messenger* to deliver this information, in full.

I speak of the beginning of the 20th century because that was when Uncle Perce was in his prime and full of beans. He not only published, in his four-page weekly, the news his fellow residents wanted, but he was sharp in the way he accomplished it. He had two main assets as a newspaper publisher and editor — his position as first selectman, which put his nose right in the middle of the main stream, and the fact that his wife (my Aunt Noan, short for Elnora), had her ear to the ground, or the telephone, on all matters and gossip outside the main stream. My aunt and uncle were the staff, except for a man who came in at press time to turn the wheel on the old, rickety press.

Aunt Noan, who did most of the typesetting, often took news items over the telephone while she was still setting type. She was the only reporter-printer I ever saw who could balance the phone on her shoulder and pick letters from the case with her right hand that she made into lines of type in the "stick" she held in her left hand — all the time listening to her informant on the other end of the telephone line tell about a "trip to Boston" or some other exciting kind of news.

She'd say, "Thanks for calling, Lil," or "Edith," or whoever and then shout to Uncle Perce, "This will fill about six inches of space. Be sure to leave room for it."

Shortly thereafter, Uncle Perce had greased the press and inked up. He was ready to (literally) grind out the week's 700 copies, printing one side of the sheet first, then the other, and later folding each by hand into the four pages of "all the news that's fit to print," at least on Deer Isle, and sometimes some that wasn't quite so fit. He called these last "my little upsetters, just to provoke a letter to the editor once in a while."

Before Uncle Perce began each Thursday's operation, however, there was one ritual that had to be performed. In the early days it seemed to go with the trade of printing. Beside the grease can under the press was a little bottle with brownish liquid in it; and Uncle Perce would reach for the bottle, take a little nip, and say, "Ready to go, Freddy. Start the press."

When I was grown enough to stand on a box and help turn the wheel, while visiting during summer vacation, I occasionally took part in getting out the weekly *Messenger*. The old press and others similar have long since disappeared. But the purpose it served is as vital today as then, the publication of news and of comments on it. Whereas Uncle Perce was not strong on editorializing, I do know that a series of his just before his passing on was considered instrumental in getting state and federal aid to build the long bridge now linking the island with the

14

mainland; he didn't live to see it actually under construction, however.

Today's newspapers, dailies and weeklies, are highly sophisticated in technological equipment, including that which makes the use of color possible. But no more fascinating color could any newspaper have than that which the old-time weekly editors provided through the individuality of their character and community involvement in the almost isolated segments of the world they functioned in — from those who were a bit pious to Uncle Perce, who wasn't.

"Ho! For the Camp Ground"

GRANDFATHER WILLIAM HOOPER would approve of what my wife and I are doing this rainy afternoon. We are repairing and framing a sign Grandfather made about a hundred years ago. We think it is high time we took this further step to help preserve it.

The sign's purpose was to drum up trade for the new four-seated buckboard that Grandfather had invented and built with his own hands. They were his hands, also, that painted the bold, black letters and the black outline of the buckboard.

Across the top of the four-foot-square piece of heavy cardboard were the words "Hooper's Beauty." In the center was the drawing, and then the bottom line said, "Ho! For the Camp Ground."

The campground was the historical area where the British camped at the time they held Castine. This town, over which four flags flew before it was secured by the American fleet, is on a peninsula. The campground site stood at the end of this peninsula.

How this sign has survived all the years is difficult to figure.

To be sure, it is brittle in places. We have had to trim the edges to get them even enough for a frame. But Grandfather's artwork is clear.

We got the sign about forty years ago from Uncle Warren. He took my wife and me up into the loft of the stable and into some rooms in the house where he had stored dozens of buffalo robes no longer needed in the dwindling livery business. There were shelves filled with bottles of horse liniment and bars of harness soap. The stable loft was the most exciting. Here was the original twenty-foot sign that had been across the stable front, just above the large doors. (Uncle Warren was using a hanging sign at the yard entrance.)

Here, also, was the little sign we are working on today. Apparently, it had been pressed between two piles of horse blankets and thus preserved. Uncle Warren's offer was quickly accepted.

We have had it on the wall, but never framed nor covered with glass. This has now been accomplished.

As I look at "Hooper's Beauty," I can see beyond the picture and the wall and into Grandfather's busy yard of his livery stable. Further, I can see the twenty-three horses in their stalls in the stable. And it is not difficult to turn left from the stable to the large carriage shed — with buckboards, phaetons, top buggies, express wagons, box buggies, and road wagons.

Grandfather would be plumb in the middle of all that was going on. I am told he was not a tall man, but lean and muscular. He had his black hair cut in a smooth crew cut, and he wore a black beard.

Before opening his livery stable, he had been a carriage maker — so it was not without justified pride that he described his newly constructed buckboard as "Hooper's Beauty."

Grandfather had three sons — Warren, who took over when Grandfather died; Will, who established his own stable but was

soon active in many business ventures; and my father, who took advantage of the normal school in Castine and went on into teaching.

Regardless of their going different ways, the Hooper brothers had one thing in common. As a result of Grandfather's insistence that they have plenty of responsibility around the stable, they were all excellent horsemen.

Although I never saw Grandfather William, I feel that I knew him through the atmosphere of the livery stable I saw so much of. His love for horses rubbed off on my father who, in turn, passed it along to me.

The sign hangs now above my typewriter. It seems natural to wave to Grandfather and to say, with vigor, "Ho! For the Camp Ground."

By Land and Sea

As SOON AS father's school in Auburn, Maine, was closed for the summer vacation, our family started getting ready for the annual trip to Castine. We would be spending the long summer at the camp father had built on Wadsworth Cove, and we would be living simply, because father's pay as principal of the Webster Grammar School did not continue through the summer.

One big trunk was sufficient for all our clothing. We didn't need much, but mother was always sure to pack a few sweaters and jackets for cool, foggy nights.

When we arrived at the railroad station to start the all-day trip, we included the cat in his basket and my pony, Xavier, in the heavy crate that father had built. The pony had been bought from my newspaper-route earnings and from whose back I could then deliver a morning and an evening route.

The American Express had picked up Xavier, and a "hired car" had delivered the rest of us to the station, father looking schoolmasterish with his pince-nez and mother perky under the little hat she had made for the occasion. We boys gleamed in our Sunday clothes and with our scrubbed faces. Mother was still dressing us alike at that time, but we had graduated from the Dutch-boy haircut. We had sailor collars on our blouses.

The gleam wouldn't last long on the sooty train, and mother gave up urging my brother and me to "stay as clean as possible for your relatives in Castine." A candy boy continuously shouting his wares up and down the train added to the difficulty of keeping sticky fingers from staining the crisp white blouses.

The train ride was always exciting, for between Lewiston and Rockland the cars would be shunted around and board a ferry. At Bath the train would be broken up into several sections, and each was pushed onto the ferry. Then, on the other side of the Kennebec River, the train would be reassembled.

Every once in a while I would go back to the freight car to see Xavier. He was not happy, but neither was he rambunctious. His usual arched neck was drooping, and his whole attitude was one of resignation. An apple now and then helped.

After hours of the train's heat, dirt, and stuffiness, we would arrive at Rockland for transfer to the boat. This was a delight, knowing that soon the salt air would sweep away the cooped-up feeling of the last several hours.

My brother and I would help mother get the bundles and suitcases onto the *Pemaquid* while father went looking for Xavier's crate and the trunk.

"He hasn't kicked the crate apart yet," father said. "Guess we'll make it if the boat doesn't roll."

The boat trip to Castine, if I remember correctly, took about two hours. These were far too short. Being on a boat is a release from everything that has been tugging at you. It is the

19

essence of unfiltered freedom. There are few joys greater than peering over the bow and watching it split the water into foam as it pushes steadily ahead.

As the *Pemaquid* approached the wharf at Dark Harbor, the only stop between Rockland and Castine, it seemed that the whole town had come down to see the boat come in. It is always fascinating to look over the ship's rail down at the faces of many types of people. The same experience was renewed for my wife and me when, a few years ago, we went by ship along the Norwegian coast. No other form of transportation attracts the gathering of townspeople as do the boats that serve coastal towns. It is a special event, breaking the daily routine.

The same welcoming crowd was on the dock when the *Pemaquid* reached Castine. It was late afternoon, and we would reach camp before dark. As we worked our way out through the crowd, Uncle Warren appeared, saying, "I've opened up the camp to let the air blow through it." He steered us to a three-seated buckboard from his livery stable for the ride to camp. There was one exception: I rode Xavier.

Xavier was the first to feel the freedom of the long summer vacation. He immediately was turned into the pasture next to the camp.

The rest of us didn't bother to unpack before going for a swim, an icy swim. The summer loomed ahead — with its raspberries, blueberries, clams, and tom-cod, which cost us nothing except time. This was part of a schoolmaster's life at that time — a happy simplicity between June and September.

Feathers and Frills

As a boy I was always fascinated that my mother made her own hats. That was at a time when all women wore hats, and most women went out and bought them. Mother made hers all through her active life, up to when she was well into her nineties. The other night on the phone I asked her why she had made her own hats for so long after it was easy to buy them.

"In the first place," she said, "my mother was a milliner and taught me how to make them as a girl. I have always enjoyed doing it and, besides, I liked what I made better than what I saw in the stores and shops. I felt I knew what looked right on me, so I made it. Saved money that way, too."

Her mother, in the 1870s in the island town of Stonington, Maine, ran a small dry-goods shop. She was an accomplished dressmaker but specialized in hats. She was a milliner, an art that wasn't every woman's cup of tea then, or now.

My grandmother instructed her daughter well, thinking that she might go into millinery instead of becoming a school-teacher. Although my mother taught her first school at the age of sixteen on a fisherman's island not far from Stonington, she continued sewing her own clothes, including her hats. That black dress form, adjusted to her size so that she could fit clothes on it, she stored in my closet, and I was forever bumping into it.

Grandmother's name was Jullietta, a rather fancy name for a Downeaster, so it is not surprising that she preferred being called Etta. She was a milliner at a time when all sewing in rural towns was done by hand and learned within the family. It was not taught in any public schools in America until the women of Boston succeeded in 1854 in having it taught in that city's schools.

The foot-operated sewing machine was a rarity, not having been patented by the Singer Manufacturing Company until 1851. The electric machine didn't come along until about 1900, again patented by Singer.

I imagine my grandmother had private instruction in

millinery, in the art of making hats. It seems amazing that in a little seacoast town of a few hundred, one of its residents could find steady work providing hats for the girls and women living on that wind-swept, ledgy island.

I asked my mother the other night if Grandmother Etta was really kept busy during those years a century ago.

"Indeed she was," mother said. "Making the hat itself took only about an hour or so, but there had to be a lot of selection of materials between her and her customer, looking over the box of feathers from Boston, choosing the cloth, deciding what style would look best on the customer."

Productions ran to two or three hats a day, and the price, a century ago, averaged about $3.00, which seems rather expensive considering what a dollar would buy at that time. It is apparent that the ladies on the island put great store in the appearance the right hat would give them in any season.

Feathers were a prominent part of headware in the late part of the nineteenth century and into the early 1900s. Some wag at that time said, "A bonnet is only an excuse for a feather." The cloth ran from velvet and heavy silks to fur and linen in season, much of it brought to this country in sailing vessels. They were frilly and had to be in order to compete with the voluminous amount of material that went into a woman's dress.

It is interesting to note that in those times a hundred years ago, when life itself was without many frills, people chose frilly clothes. In these modern days of flashy automobiles and neon lights, the clothes women wear, including the few hats, are relatively simple. The town milliner is a thing of the past.

The human body has emerged almost as nature made it. Heads are unadorned and women's hair in many cases is cut shorter than men's.

One can't help wondering why in the frugal, simple, and relatively quiet living style of a century ago fashion decreed that women wear as many as three petticoats at a time and hats that were plaited with velvet flowers.

The Horseback Lesson

BACK AT THE TURN of the century a housewife's life was pretty much in a groove. There was washing on Monday, ironing on Tuesday, mending on Wednesday, and each day had its routine. My mother, who has always had a streak of independence in her and still does in her 103d year, had no intention of getting into this groove when she left schoolteaching and married a fellow teacher. She felt that a wife should have enough flexibility in her daily life to do things with her husband when circumstances arose. Her philosophy was that a happy marriage called for sharing as many activities as possible in which there was a common interest.

As principal of the high school, my father earned $450 for the school year. To supplement his income in the summer he drove an express wagon delivering baggage from the arriving boats. If he passed by the house on a fine day and thought mother would enjoy riding along with him, and if she happened to be frying doughnuts at the time, she would put the fat on the back of the stove and go along with him. They could have the doughnuts together at the end of the day.

One of the things my mother was determined to do in those early days of her marriage, some seventy-five years ago, was to learn some of the outdoor sports my father enjoyed. One of these was horseback riding, even though she was frightened to death of horses. Father, having been brought up in a livery-stable atmosphere, still liked to get onto a horse as often as possible.

Mother thought that she could put her fear aside and learn to enjoy this activity with him. As in most things, she was a woman of determination — she took up golf when she was in her late fifties and learned to drive a car at the same time so she could get to the golf course and practice.

When she decided to get ready for her first horseback lesson, she was aware that in those days one had to be properly dressed for the occasion. A woman's legs had to be covered. This meant making herself a riding skirt.

She found a pattern for a divided riding skirt and set about making it. First she laid the pattern on a table, but the legs of the skirt were so large that she had to transfer it to the kitchen floor. As soon as she discovered which was the top and which the bottom, she proceeded to cut it.

The next step was to sew it up and try it on. Having spent considerable time before reaching this point, and her knees cramped from turning and twisting the pattern around, she got up from the floor with even less enthusiasm for horseback riding than she had started with.

With my father helping, she finally got into it, but there was something radically wrong. It was so voluminous that she had sewed the top of one side to the bottom of the other. There was nothing to do but rip it out and start over again. She picked up the scissors and handed my father another pair.

It was finished the next morning, and Mother found that she could get into it and walk around but wondered if she could sit on it. She had no desire whatsoever to find that out on a real horse, so she went out into the barn and straddled a saw horse. There she found that she had room enough in the seat and that the legs were the right length.

Everything was ready for the horseback lesson.

They rode into a park and she managed to stay on, probably because the skirt held her on. In fact she was doing so well that father suggested she could ride back to the stable through Main Street and could enter the stable yard at a trot.

24

"Well, I started to trot," mother used to say, "and I gathered speed every minute. I began to scream. The louder I screamed the faster the horse trotted and the higher I bounced. He ran right into the barn, came to a sliding halt in his stall, and I found myself looking straight into the rack he ate his hay from. I decided right then and there to let him eat all the hay he wanted thereafter. I could find somebody who could use that divided skirt."

As far as I know, this is the only time her determination deserted her. Some people are born allergic to horses.

Father Did the Food Shopping

THERE WAS A TIME when the pay for teaching school was much lower, proportionately, than that of other skilled or professional workers. The older teachers don't have to be told this. Many of the younger teachers may have no idea what the difference was in the relative incomes of the times.

For a father in a family of four, the fact that he was principal of a grammar school did not relieve him from the struggle to make ends meet. He had to be very careful with his small salary.

It was good for my family that my father was a meticulous man. By being a watcher of details he could stretch the use of his earnings during the school year, from stocking up during sales of tinned goods to buying only quality clothes whose extra durability would help keep him neat in his job over several years. It was his theory, for instance, that by alternating two pairs of Stetson shoes it was possible for the unused pair to respond to proper leather treatment.

He also found it cheaper to buy two tailor-made suits at a time, made from cloth that was as durable as iron.

This isn't where he really proved he could afford to enjoy teaching in spite of what the taxpayers were willing to pay for his professional dedication to the job. His greatest secret, in general, was careful food shopping. His specific secret was his knowledge of meat, the quality cuts that provided more meat for the money than those at a lower price.

When he was going to Eastern State Normal School, up in Castine, Maine, he learned meat cutting in Uncle Frank's market. Later, when it was time to provide for a family in Auburn, where he spent forty years as a school principal, he soon proved to the best meat markets in the twin cities of Auburn and Lewiston that he knew meat.

It didn't take long, after a conversation with the meat-cutter in any market before the man behind the counter got tired of the detailed questions and brought out the cut father really wanted. It got so that in several markets, he was invited to come out back and cut his own. The market man evidently felt he saved time that way.

We ate well, "high on the hog," as they say, yet it was an economical table and one a teacher could afford. Further, by being a school principal who kept in close touch with the students, he was able to learn from time to time when one of the farmer fathers was butchering a calf. Thus, by going to the source, he was able to add delicious calf's liver. Often the farm boy would deliver it directly to the school, where the lunch room had an icebox.

It may be that he could do as well in some small markets today. However, the miles of display shelves and barricades of glass and brick in the larger supermarkets would have been frustrating, I am sure, to his kind of personal selection.

Unfortunately, I don't know the kind of cuts he favored, nor did I acquire any of his astuteness in this field.

Knowing what he was talking about was an asset to him in

26

several different fields. His junior high school, one of the first in Maine in a new building, which replaced his old grammar school down by the railroad tracks, was a laboratory for the education department of nearby Bates College. He never had a college degree, and didn't want one, but he was a creator of what college professors recognized as a stimulating advance in public education.

Because he had need for supplementary income, and although he had never played football, he studied the game and for a number of years was a respected football official for the four Maine colleges.

A man with a mathematical mind, he became engrossed in card games. His ability at poker, which few of the taxpaying public in Auburn knew about, paid my tuition for my freshman year at Bates College.

Father ran an orderly, relaxed but disciplined school. There were rules, and they meant what they said. Whether it was the times or a reflection of his own interest and pride in the school, there were few occasions for resorting to disciplinary action. The penalties existed, and it was known that they would be applied if necessary.

Teachers' salaries were based on the school year in which they worked. The long summers were either a vacation or a time to find supplementary jobs. My father chose, in the early years of our family, to build a camp near the shore on his brother's Castine farm. It was a case of living off the land or from the clam flats and cove down front. To this, he added tutoring rich summer kids on the estates around town.

He still did what food shopping was necessary, getting to know what fishermen were due in at what hour, or rowing out to the herring weir in our cove. Berries were in abundance for the picking, of course, and milk with cream came free for helping with the cows and doing the haying on Uncle Warren's farm.

He did have one favorite lobsterman who always threw an extra one or two into the pail. Big Ed had a slight impediment in his speech and called his catch "robsters."

Come to think of it, that's what anybody today might find himself calling this scarce and costly product of the sea.

Rust in Peace

A TROLLEY CAR might look a bit awkward when seen beside today's streamlined train or sleekly engineered automobiles. To those of us who enjoyed the convenience of trolley cars, however, this kind of transportation had its own beauty.

Literally, the blunt-nosed trolleys didn't have to be ungainly and homely. By use of color, gold-painted letters, and even striped awnings on each side of the car, many trolleys acquired an attractiveness of their own — as contrasted with dump carts and even the trains of their days.

On occasion, I rode the trolley car to get my newspapers for my route. This was only, however, when I was late. I preferred to walk and save the nickel.

Later, it was a trolley that brought the papers for my morning route. I met the car at 5:30 A.M. with my pony. The same conductor was always on the car, and he would invariably greet me with: "Good morning, Johnny Sun-up." The name of the newspaper was the *Morning Sun*, too.

When I was in my father's grammar school, our baseball team played those in nearby towns. By the time the season was half over, the trolley company had shifted from the closed car to the summer open ones. The seats went all the way across the car and there was a running-board on each side. When the car would pull into the town whose grammar-school team we were going to play, we would raise our voices in a chant: "Before the sun goes down, in any old town, Webster will win." Our coach, Arthur Marsten, had taught us to do this. I suppose he felt it might help, in an intimidating way. Heaven knows, the team I was on could use any help it could get.

As a means of transportation, a trolley car had a definite rhythm. The sound of the tireless metal wheels on the metal track (laid in pieces that left a slight gap between each separate length of track) was well caught in these lines from an old song: "I am coming, I am coming, hark you hear my motor running; for the trolley's come to conquer, so you cannot keep it back."

The trolley car dates back to the 1890s, but it was the decade after the turn of the century that brought the trolley into full flower. Connecting towns as it did, and serving cities by connecting neighborhoods to the central business area, the trolley's flexibility was notable when it became the means of getting people to the parks and recreational areas. Trolley management promoted the parks, for obvious reasons, and then cashed in on them once they had become attractive.

Just as many courtships took place in the buggies of the horse-and-buggy days, many also doubtless were carried on in the trolleys that served the parks and their open-air dance floors.

Where else, also, would a high-school picnic find its transportation to the lake or to the fairgrounds if not on an open trolley car?

In existence, still, is the expression, "It tastes like the inside of a motorman's glove." This had its origin in the fact that the motorman in the front of the car constantly had one gloved hand grasping the top of a metal handle with which he controlled the speed of the car. Being "electric cars," the handle controlled the power from the wire above the tracks, the power coming through the trolley running on the wire and transmitted to the car's motor.

Quite as I would be pleased with a return to the horse-drawn vehicles, I also feel that I saw too little of the era of the trolley car.

The Soothing Mrs. Winslow

IN 1871 TWO PRESTIGIOUS firms, Jeremiah Curtin and Sons of New York and London and John J. Brown and Sons of Boston and London, were jointly interested in making sure that anyone with a cough, cold, or sore throat should obtain relief by purchasing a bottle of Mrs. Winslow's Soothing Syrup.

Their faith in their product was not tainted by modesty. There was no substitute for Mrs. Winslow's. "All others are base imitations."

To further their cause they published a recipe book. Its authorship was attributed to "Mrs. Winslow," but its several hundred recipes in the little four-by-seven pamphlet obviously were common to most New England tables in that period of more than a century ago.

It starts off with a useful suggestion for its readers, just in case they are out of yeast at the very minute they want to roll the dough. "Make milk yeast," Mrs. Winslow says. "Take one pint of new milk, one teaspoon of salt, one tablespoon of flour stirred in, stand in a kettle of water by the stove and keep it lukewarm all the time. When very light, add lukewarm water, make into loaves or biscuit, and let them rise by the fire before cooking."

Who needs yeast?

Maybe you haven't had any Sweet Rusks lately. You can make them by taking "one quart new milk, three tablespoons yeast [you have been able to get to your grocer's by this time], flour to make a thick batter; mix at night, and in the morning

30

add one cup fresh lard and one cup of sugar rubbed together; three eggs, well-beaten, preserving the white of one, beaten to a stiff froth, with a little sugar to spread over the tops — Excellent. Try them."

Mrs. Winslow goes heavily into desserts — indicating that calorie counting wasn't a dominant factor in diet a century ago.

One of her lighter offerings is apple float. "To one quart of apples partially stewed and well mashed, put the white of three eggs well-beaten and four heaping tablespoons loaf sugar; beat them together fifteen minutes, and eat with cream and nutmeg."

There's a veal pie in this little book that was recently found in an old attic. Maybe with today's prices and scarcity of veal, it would be well to leave the veal pie in the dusty book. But if you are curious, this is how it was prepared for earlier tables: "Take a shoulder of veal, cut it up and boil one hour, then add a quarter pound of butter, pepper and salt, cover the meat with biscuit dough, cover close and stew half an hour — and it will be ready."

If I can get hold of one of the little pigs some young neighbors have started to raise for next winter's freezer, I am going to try this recipe of Mrs. Winslow's: "Pig's Head Baked — Let it be divided and thoroughly cleaned; take out the brains, trim the snout and ears, bake it an hour and a half, wash the brains thoroughly; blanch them, beat them up with an egg, pepper and salt, and some finely chopped or pounded sage, and small piece of butter, fry or brown them before the fire; serve with the head."

In addition to her recipes, Mrs. Winslow has numerous household hints. among them is this advice on how to remove stains from the hands: "A few drops of oil vitriol (sulfuric acid) in water will take the stains of fruit, dark dyes, stove blacking, etc., from the hands without injuring them. Care must, however, be taken not to drop it upon the clothes. It will remove the color from woolen, and eat holes in cotton fabrics."

Mrs. Winslow's Recipe Book, according to its publishers, was issued annually. Readers were urged to preserve them and sew them together. Thus, it was noted, "you will have in a few years the best collection of recipes in the country."

Hopefully, during that time also, Messrs. Brown and Curtis would be able to sell you many bottles of Mrs. Winslow's Soothing Syrup and many packages of Brown's Bronchial Trockies: "All others are base imitations."

Learning by Earning

WHEN DESCRIBING ONE'S EDUCATION, it is customary to list the schools attended and degrees, if any, earned. There is more to education, however, than schools can provide. One of those forms of extra education is the way a boy or girl earned money during those years of formal schooling.

I don't know whether young people have more, or less, opportunity to work today. I do know that some fifty years ago there seemed to be a way to earn money if the youngster wanted to work. At least that's my recollection.

What got me started on this subject was coming across a King air rifle in the boy's closet. I started to figure how old it was and remembered that I had got it sixty-five years ago by sending in a bunch of wrappers from Castile soap.

This all came about from my first effort to earn money. I became an agent for Castile soap, which I carried around the neighborhood in a cart. I asked my customers to save the wrappers for me, and I picked them up once a week. I sent these wrappers to get the King air rifle. Sixty-five years haven't dulled its spring mechanism a bit, and it still shoots reasonably straight. In fact, it is in better shape than I am.

Well, now we've started a march of jobs while growing up. Can't stop with the first one. What were the second and third?

They were the newspaper routes on which I learned the importance of keeping records, the patience to keep after the slow payers, and to begin to understand some of the differences among people. Of all the jobs I had as a youth, I think having a newspaper route left more of a mark, educationally, than any other work. The reason, probably, was because of the responsibility involved. You carried the route. You collected. There was nobody to do it for you.

Another kind of job I held was extremely fascinating. One winter while in grammar school, I delivered milk every morning from 5:30 until it was time to run to school. The route was slower on Saturdays because the man who owned the farm made his collections then.

It was cold, and I usually ran along beside the sleigh to keep warm. On Saturday I drove the horse, almost enough of a joy to make me willing to work for nothing.

Quite a different job became available when I hit my teens. I donned a white apron and stepped behind the counter in an S. K. Ames Butter, Cheese and Egg store. Here, the need was to learn a skill as rapidly as possible. The skill was to cut a pound of cheese that was a pound, give or take an ounce. The same was true with butter. The coffee didn't have to be cut but it did have to be ground (from the bean) to suit the customer. And it did smell good.

From S. K. Ames, my other big store job was behind the shirt counter in Peck's Department Store, which lacked the coziness of the butter-and-egg environment. It's not just that the shirts all looked alike to me, but in the pre-Christmas season there were two weeks of twelve-hour days. That kind of weariness and boredom I had never known before.

The two summers in my Uncle Fred's grocery store were helpful in providing a different kind of responsibility. This came from the fact that I was outside the store delivering — and driving to the wholesaler's in Rockland.

When I first went to work for Uncle Fred, his clerk greeted me as follows: "Hello there. I'm Bill Heald. Do you live around here or do you ride a bicycle?" I'm still trying to figure out how to answer that one.

While attending Bates College, I had my first taste of newspaper reporting. This comprised reporting college events, and local student news, for the *Lewiston Evening Journal* — one of the papers I had worked for as a carrier.

34

During the summers, while in college, I got to know different forms of recreational and tourist facilities. At King and
Bartlett lakes I tutored the son and daughter of the camp's
owners. The fact that part of the job was being postmaster,
which required occasional trips from the camp to Eustis, fifteen
miles through the forest. The road was a log tote road—testing
every ounce of the buckboard.

The following summer I worked at the Oak Bluffs House at
a mixture of jobs—menu printer, fire builder in the morning,
and bus driver to the boat. At Oak Bluffs I met John "Floppo"
Allen, who was in charge of supplies. Over a period of time he
convinced me to transfer to Wesleyan University, his college.
What sold me was the chance to study under the Maine poet
Wilbert Snow. That move, I figure, was the real bonus added
to the meager pay at the hotel. Who would ever tip a menu
printer?

Floppo Allen gave me the best tip.

Knee-Deep in Daisies

REMEMBER WHEN YOU STOOD in front of a big glass candy
case and reached up to point to the Tootsie Rolls? "Please, mis-
ter, I want two of those." And you got two for a penny.

This morning, as I was buying my *New York Times,* I found
Tootsie Rolls staring back at me. This was no mirage. It was
for real.

This took me back about 55 years to the corner grocery in
Auburn, where I was in the habit of doing my candy shopping.
Perhaps the penny came from the ten cents allowance I got from
my father every Saturday. It wasn't strictly an allowance, for I
had to feed the hens every day in order to get my weekly payoff.
I have been allergic to the very thought of hens ever since.

35

Let's say that while I was unwrapping one of the Tootsie Rolls I was waiting for the electric street car in order to go to the movie across the Androscoggin River in Lewiston. As I remember then, the Tootsies were softer than those I bought this morning. Be that as it may, I had a sweet Tootsie tucked into my cheek when the trolley came along. I was pleased that the seat just behind the motorman was empty, because this gave me a chance to watch him operate the car.

In Lewiston, I got off at the Nickel, so named because that was the going price for entering its dark interior—where your hair might be made to stand on end as what is known as "violence" today was rolled before your eyes.

The movie that day was *Iron Claw,* chapters of which had been running for weeks. Each chapter was a story in itself but it ended with a teaser to bring you back the next week.

On that Saturday afternoon, along with several hundred other kids and a few adults, I witnessed the hero undergo many harrowing dangers as the villain, the Iron Claw, thoroughly messed up the hero's pursuit of happiness. Finally, he was chased to the edge of a cliff some 2,000 feet above a rocky shore. There we left him, hanging not by his fingers but by his fingernails. The lights went on just as the words "17th Episode Next Week" appeared on the screen.

After the movie, my mother met me in Union Square to go buy a new suit, which I would need for the recital of Professor Testor's clarinet class. (There were twenty of us in the class at the same time—mass production of artists!) We went to the boys department in Pecks.

I was annoyed that mother didn't feel I was old enough for long trousers. So I came out of Pecks with a navy blue suit comprising a short jacket (for Buster Brown collar) and pants that came to just above the knees. They would be worn with black socks that came to just below the knee.

Speaking of Professor Testor's clarinet class—my brother "took" violin in a class about the same size. I have never known why neither of us ever advanced beyond the beginner's level. It could have been the size of those classes, which precluded individual instruction, or it could have been lack of talent. I fear it was the latter.

On the day we are talking about, mother apparently thought that my disappointment over not getting long trousers might be lightened with some sort of gift. She settled on one the whole family could enjoy. Incidentally, mother was an accomplished guitarist and couldn't see why her musical capacities didn't rub off on her two sons.

Before going home on the trolley we went back to Peck's music department. There, among the pianos, mandolins, guitars, and clarinets, she bought a record by Whispering Jack Smith called "Knee-Deep in Daisies."

It was good to get home where I could hear the new record on our Victrola. Only I still had to feed the hens before I could sit down and listen.

Going Home

DURING MY MOTHER'S CHILDHOOD in Stonington, Maine, transportation between the coastal towns was by horse and carriage or by boat. She had faith in the safety of boats, having made a number of trips with her father whose coastal schooner, a hundred years ago, carried granite from Stonington to Boston.

There came a day, however, at the end of her first term at Castine Normal School, when her faith in boats was tested as it had never been before. She had never been at sea before in a snowstorm.

It was not uncommon for the girls training to be teachers at the normal school to charter a boat to take them to their homes at vacation time. For those who lived on the coast, this was the normal thing to do.

So, in anticipation of being home for Thanksgiving, about 30 of them gathered at the wharf. It was cold and the gray clouds were hanging low. There was a spit of snow in the air.

The excited young women, warmed against the cold by their long underwear tucked down into their cotton stockings and further protected by flannel petticoats, eagerly awaited the arrival of the steamer *Castine,* a fair-sized boat some 70 feet long and 25 feet deep.

The snow increased, and the school's principal came down to the wharf to persuade the group not to go. He pointed out that coastal snowstorms sometimes turn to blizzards, and they shouldn't take that chance.

But they were young and had no fears — if the captain thought it was all right.

At last they heard the captain say, "Well, I'm going anyway, for I have to be at Bar Harbor tonight."

Most of the girls knew the captain, who was a frequent visitor to their towns. They knew he had followed the sea all his life, and since they had not been forbidden to make the trip, they decided to go.

They moved out of the harbor in a mild snowstorm. But after they had been at sea for about an hour, the storm grew worse and heavy waves began to beat against the side of the boat. The air was white with snow.

Many of the girls were sick and others too frightened to be sick. A few of those who had had some rough trips at sea before were still on deck, watching the rollers and watching the captain take them head-on with his boat. Among those braver ones was my mother, feeling the security she had always experienced on her father's vessel.

Suddenly the waves began to sweep the deck. They were all ordered below into the cabin. From there on, it was a steady uproar. Tables and chairs were tossed from one side of the floor to the other. Girls screamed.

They realized they were well out into the ocean, out of sight of land. They were being tossed about like feathers. Each wave that now hit the boat seemed about to tear it apart. By this time, everybody was frantic, even my mother, as she told us some years later.

When one of the girls fainted and failed to react to treatment, one of the crewmen crawled along the deck to the pilot house for advice from the captain.

"Don't ask a thing," said the captain. "If I leave this pilot house for a minute you'll all be drowned."

The trip raged on for another hour, until the captain brought his boat into Seal Harbor.

For the young students, it had been an eventful trip home for Thanksgiving.

The Unlikely Brothers

I HAD TWO UNCLES who were so different that a stranger never would have suspected such close blood relationship, except for the Hooper nose. I probably was aware of the differences, as a boy, but from this distance I can see far better how unlike these two Maine brothers were. They come back into my mind at this moment because I was thinking how little the basic qualities of human nature change, with some still getting strong emphasis in one individual, while other basic quirks of human nature dominate other individuals.

Fashions, customs, and technological and social environments have changed over the years, but people, basically, haven't changed very much. That's why I am using these two uncles of my boyhood in reflecting on some of the qualities of human nature I still see around me.

Uncle Will and Uncle Warren grew up in the atmosphere of my grandfather's livery stable opposite the Customs House at Castine, Maine, a summer resort town that had a population in the winter of about 400, swollen to about 1,500 when the "summer folks" occupied their spacious houses and filled the harbor with boats.

Uncle Warren was lean, slow in movement, and one to whom time meant little. He was always ready for conversation but was a poor planner of a day's work. Uncle Will was built something like a Kewpie Doll but with great dignity, always planning and with little time for conversation other than that which had to do with his many enterprises. This was when they were in their prime — Uncle Warren in the heavy woolen pants he wore winter and summer, Uncle Will in starched collar, white shirt, and the blue-and-white pin-striped trousers that were his trademark.

After Grandfather died, they had started operating the livery stable together. But only for a short time, for Uncle Will decided to set up his own livery stable on the waterfront, thinking he would attract livery passengers more quickly being near the visiting yachts. Once on the waterfront, he started to acquire the whole of it, bit by bit. He set up a coal business and an ice business, bought the steamboat wharf, and after a while became one of the first Model-T Ford dealers on the Maine coast. Somehow or other, he also became an undertaker.

One day he was rocking on his front porch with a friend, and I was perched on the rail listening. Uncle Will, out of the corner of his eye, saw an old man walking past. "Hmm," he said, "Henry's getting kind of feeble. Tall man, too. Wonder if I've got a casket that will fit him."

In the meantime, Uncle Warren operated the old livery stable and a farm several miles out of town. When the moon was bright, he'd delay his milking so as to watch the moonlight playing on the bay nearby. Even though the development of the automobile ate into his livery business, he felt it was only "temporary." Finally he stored all his carriages, buffalo robes, and livery equipment—selling some, years later, to Ford's Dearborn Museum, which not too many years ago was destroyed by fire.

Uncle Will died during the years Uncle Warren was waiting for the livery business to come back. On one beautiful June day my wife and I stopped in to see him. "Beautiful day, Uncle Warren," we said. "Yes," he replied, "but I dread the winter."

Finally, Uncle Warren went to live with a son in Akron, Ohio. He had long wanted to see the Kentucky Derby. So, in his eighties, he bundled himself one day into his old woolen coat, which came down to his ankles like the linen dusters early car drivers wore, and set off from Akron by bus to the Derby. It just happened to be one of the coldest days on which the Derby ever had been run, and, among the thousands attending that Southern unique test of the best in horse racing, Uncle Warren was about the only one properly dressed for it.

Although he was not to live long after that, the old man who had always felt the world should have stuck to horses had completed his life's cycle with the fulfillment of a desire to see with his own eyes the place and the event where horses not only were still important but for a few hours, at least, overshadowed everything else.

Two brothers, but very different men. Who can say which had the more satisfying life?

Parsnips? Never

AROUND THE YEARS of 1915–18, boys just under their teens in northern New England were expected to find ways of earning their own spending money and, in many cases, their clothes money. I don't know about the girls. In the elementary schools, the boys' side and the girls' side of the yard were separate. Where the girls were seemed to be made mostly of squeals.

Among my own ways of helping earn my keep, besides a newspaper route, were selling Castile soap in the neighborhood and assisting the milkman on Saturday mornings, because that was the day he collected for his week's deliveries. In the winter, this meant running alongside the long sled to keep warm. I guess this is the way the horse kept warm, too, up front of the heavy milk sled.

The milkman wore a fur coat that came to his ankles, probably made of muskrat skins. One of the ways I earned money in 1917 was trapping muskrats along a brook not far from home, where it was possible to tend my traps every morning before going to school.

In case you are not familiar with muskrats, they looked less like rats and more like small beavers, except they had the long, rodentlike tail. They were plentiful, and their glossy brown fur was popular, as well as inexpensive, for both men's and women's fur coats.

I really was not cut out to be a trapper. I was a softie and hated to harm an animal. But there it was, a way to earn money.

The trap was a vicious little clamp-jaw affair. It was set, however, in a special way to be as humane as possible. This meant placing it on a board beside the brook's bank in a way that would assure the trapped muskrat a sudden fall into the brook where he would expire quickly under the water. I carried a .22 rifle, just in case a trap hadn't accomplished what it was supposed to and the muskrat would still be alive when I got to him in the early morning. One of those days was my undoing as a trapper.

I looked at the muskrat and he looked at me, then I looked at my gun. I had never shot an animal, only targets. The rifle, aimed at the muskrat, seemed to be mounted on a swivel, with me as the swivel. The barrel moved in a circle. The muskrat seemed to be disgusted with the shaking boy standing in front of him. I don't know how many shots it took to hit the target, but the ordeal eventually was over. It was perhaps during those tense moments that a boy had his first lesson in compassion. Why is it that so many of the human virtues have to be learned the hard way?

Prior to this notable morning I had successfully trapped many muskrats and taught myself to skin them as simply a job that had to be done. I had mounted the stretched skins on boards and cured them during a period when they hung all over the walls of the back shed. My mother didn't think this collection was the best thing to have ornamenting a part of the premises where the odor of musk was at times a bit heavy.

The next step in this home business was perhaps more of a test of a boy's inner strength than any part of the trapping itself. The skins had to be sold to the local fur dealer in order to make the whole business worthwhile.

Mr. Eldridge was a burly man with a full, drooping mustache almost as though someone had hung a glossy brown muskrat skin under his nose. He was gruff and had little sympathy for the small trapper standing in his shop with his arms full of brown skins.

"Come now, boy, let's have a look at them," he would bark. Quickly examining each skin to judge the fur and to see if small hands had left any tears and cuts, he would make his offer.

"Gee, Mr. Eldridge, after all this work this is what you will pay me?" was usually the first part of a conversation that would go back and forth until my shoulders slumped and I gave in to the few pennies he had added to his original offer.

What I was paid didn't seem like much, even then, but it did mean the new black and red Mackinaw jacket my heart had been set on all during my weeks of daily visits to my trap line.

There was a hangover to this enterprise that had stayed with me for many years. My traps were baited with parsnips to which I added the bottled scent that would attract the furry animal. The scent was far from alluring to me. I have never been able to eat parsnips. Not ever!

The Great Pony Race

A SHETLAND PONY named Xavier was for several years during my childhood the most important reason for my being alive and happy. He was the focal point of my existence and will probably crop up occasionally in my writing.

I never thought much of how we got together or how far he had traveled. I knew I wanted a pony and had saved newsboy earnings to buy one. Uncle Warren had written from his livery stable at Castine, Maine, that he had recently visited Belfast, across the bay, and had talked with a horse dealer who had a black Shetland stallion for sale. Should he go further?

All I knew then was that he had come from Belfast to Auburn, and originally from the Shetland Islands. Not until I read an article recently in the *New York Times,* datelined "Scallaway, Shetland Islands," did I realize how lucky I was to have a pony born in those rocky, wind-swept islands north of Scotland. In the more than sixty years since Xavier arrived to become a part of an American boy's life, the export market from that group of small islands has dwindled to almost nothing. One reason is that it now costs about $1,400 to fly a six-month-old colt to this country. I paid less than $100 for Xavier, outright.

The Shetland Islands now have only about 1,000 brood mares and a few dozen stallions to produce the few colts for export. These tiny horses are, if pure-bred, built like horses. The proportions are the same, just smaller. They have always been distinguished by long manes and tails. The stallions had thicker manes and tails and beautifully arched necks.

In their native haunts in those North Atlantic islands they were usually shaggy. Under my relentless but happy grooming, Xavier wore a dappled dark-light black in all but the coldest Maine weather.

In that period, and reaching into the 1920s, ponies and horses were more for boys than girls. Now it is the opposite — watch the horse shows.

In my newsboy days, aside from the work Xavier and I did on evening and morning routes, we joined other boys on pony-club trips or Cowboy and Indian games or just plain exploring the hills. We did have one girl in the club, but she was an out-and-out tomboy.

Over several years, Xavier collected his share of blue ribbons at the state fair in Lewiston. He should have. He was a beautiful animal with registry papers proving him one of the best of the breed. You don't see many like him today, if any.

I never regretted the hours I spent taking care of him, sometimes in the bitter cold, chopping away to clean out the stall and spread fresh shavings. I enjoyed every minute driving him or on his back. Except once.

It had been rumored that the Lewiston fair was going to put on a pony race in September.

"This," I said to Xavier, "is our chance. No more ribbons for you looking handsome. You are going to race for one."

I picked out a half-mile stretch of back road, the distance around the track at the fairgrounds, and we trained. He liked sports but got bored with distance. I had to do a lot of coaxing, a lot of talking. He had a way of cocking one ear back to hear what I was saying, and if he didn't like it he would push both of them forward again.

The day came for the big race. I had to start early in the morning to ride him to the fairgrounds, but the race was an extra event set for early afternoon.

It seemed as though a hundred of us lined up, just beyond the big grandstand. The distance was to be not quite a half-mile, after all.

Anyhow, we were soon given the shouted word and were on our way. Xavier seemed to be enjoying it, running close to the ground with his nose thrust straight ahead. We covered half the course in that manner, and in the front ranks.

I began to think we could do better. I dug my heels into him, gave him the bit square in his teeth on a loose rein and said, "Let's beat 'em, Zave."

We were turning into the final stretch. I swung Xavier to the outside to pass as many as possible. Suddenly I noticed the main gate to the track was open just ahead of us, but thought nothing of it. Xavier did.

He took an abrupt right turn through the gate. I went straight ahead on our previous course, not on Xavier but flying through the air and finally flat into the dusty track.

I picked myself up and started looking for the missing pony. A long time later I found him milling around the midway like any of the other attractions in that area. When I got up to him I simply said, "Let's go home."

Again it was a long ride to the stable; but it was not half as long as the look Xavier gave me as I took his bridle off and turned him toward his box stall. His look said just one thing.

46

Rather, it asked just one question: "Why did you get me into that mess in the first place?"

We stuck to delivering newspapers after that.

Patent Leather Pumps

THERE I SAT in my dark knee-length pants and short jacket with Buster Brown collar. I was huddled as far down into the seat as possible, because the trolley car was packed with people. I was hoping that none of my fellow newsboys would see me.

I was on my way to dancing school.

I had already carried my papers on my beginner's route, a neighborhood one given boys before they were old enough to take on a larger route. The bundle of papers was dropped off a trolley car about the same time that I got home from school.

Once a week, during the dancing-school period of several weeks, I would rush around my small route, change my clothes, and head for dancing school. The boys whom I didn't want to be seen by on my trolley-car ride were those I met each Saturday in the newspaper alley when I settled my weekly accounts. I had received a bloody nose on more than one occasion on these Saturday junkets to the newspaper's circulation office.

To have been seen by certain contemporaries, all dressed up for that dancing class, would have been the basis for later taunting. By most of them it was considered "sissy."

Some parents, among them mine, felt that learning to dance at an early age was important. It was like getting a child interested in a musical instrument, whether he was musical or not. It was the proper thing to do, to set a child on the right track among the finer things of life. At dancing school, he might at least get some added instruction in good manners.

47

Arriving at the big brick building whose third floor housed "Professor" Pendleton's ballroom dancing class, I slowly trudged up the flights of dirty stairs and entered the bleak room.

Quickly slipping on my shiny patent leather pumps, I took my seat with some twenty other ten-year-old boys lined up on one side of the room. We faced an approximately equal number of girls exactly opposite us on the other side. Neat as pins, tightly curled, and with hands folded in the laps of their very best dresses, they stared back at us. How much unhappiness was stored at the moment in that high-ceilinged room nobody will ever know. It was not like going to a party. It was a chore to be endured for exactly one hour.

Complete silence filled the room, even though Mrs. Pendleton was already seated at the piano, smiling and waiting for her husband's triumphant entrance.

Suddenly he was in the middle of the floor, in his Prince Albert coat and his arms raised above his head as he bowed, first to one side and then the other.

"Welcome again, my young friends," he said loudly. "Tonight we again waltz. Young gentlemen, you may choose your partners — the girl sitting opposite you, first."

We boys moved out, I trying to keep my eyes on the girl I figured was "opposite." Naturally, there was confusion.

"Come, come," shouted the Professor. "Remember, you are young gentlemen. No running."

Somebody else had taken the "opposite" girl I was supposed to have bowed to. So, I ended up with a girl near her, more than a head taller than I. We all stood waiting for the next order.

"Place your right hand gently in the middle of your young lady's back. With your left hand clasp the young lady's right hand and both bend your elbows slightly. We are now ready." The "professor" nodded to his wife, whose hands then struck the waltz chords on the piano. I think the piece was "The Beautiful Blue Danube." What else?

"One, two, three. One, two, three. Slide, don't hop. Glide like a swan." And thus the struggle went on, with many more little hopping chickens than gliding swans.

Their stiff pattern and formality were part of the times. They were as uncomfortable as the trolley cars that transported these little holders of patent leather pumps.

Thunder and Lightning

I DON'T KNOW how you feel about thunderstorms, but they make me uneasy. We've just had one of our typical storms here in the southeast of Vermont. By typical, I mean that the storms hereabouts peck away at us from all sides, as though they can't make up their mind just where to zero in. Part of the reason is the abundance of hills along the Connecticut River valley.

In contrast was Uncle Perce's house down in Maine. It was on the highest part of the island, and when a storm rolled in it was headed for Uncle Perce. It seemed to know which room he would be sitting in.

This time we were sitting at the supper table. We had just reached the dessert, which was one of Aunt Noan's luscious blueberry pies. Aunt Noan, as usual, was talking. Suddenly there was a clap of thunder, which shook the house and brought with it a bouncing chain of lightning that skittered across the floor. Aunt Noan didn't miss a beat in what she was saying. But Aunt Selma, past whose feet the lightning went, was as white as a ghost.

We boys, my brother and I, felt it was a good show but a little too close for comfort.

During our childhood summers on the Maine coast we experienced many storms that seemed to engulf the house and that struck trees all around it. I am sure they were more severe, more intense, than those which play around our hills here in Vermont. To be sure, we have had some sharp ones, but on the whole their bark is worse than their bite. There is always the exception to the rule, however, and the exceptions remain vivid.

The mountains around here didn't deter one storm that arrived with great fury and seemed reluctant to move on. We had sat through the evening wondering if this one would ever let up. My wife decided to go to bed and was in the bedroom when a shattering sound seemed to be tearing the house apart. She screamed and came through the bedroom door with her clothes around her feet. It took a little while before we both were convinced that lightning had not struck the house.

The other exception to our tentative storms was when we were sitting a storm out in the living room. It wasn't a storm that could be ignored. We were discussing our experiences with thunderstorms, and Aunt Selma, who was visiting, told about the lightning playing around her feet years ago at Uncle Perce's.

Just then a roar of thunder engulfed the house, and a streak of lightning whizzed past her feet. I haven't the slightest idea where it entered the house or where it went. It simply was the second time I had seen a ball of light pass Aunt Selma during a thunderstorm. Only her, nobody else.

I am sure these recollections of thunderstorms are not as dramatic as those which many readers have experienced. However varied our experiences, I am sure we all share the feeling of the unpredictability of this natural phenomenon. In spite of all that science has provided in explanation of weather, each thunderstorm retains elements of mystery. Each creates its own uncertainty until it has completed its course.

My Uncle Will was a man who avoided profanity. If he felt

the need for swearing he would usually show it by using the word "thunderation." "Where in thunderation have you been," for instance. If he were very upset, he would say, "Thunder and lightning, that isn't what I wanted." In between was "by thunder."

The expressions seem to have disappeared, but thunder and lightning have not.

Edna Millay's Mother

SHE WAS THE MOTHER of poets, but more important to her was having her yeast delivered on time to do her bread-baking every other day. At that time she lived alone in the hills up back of Camden, Maine. I was the one whose job it was to get her yeast to her when she needed it.

This was some 50 years ago, and I was driving a Model-T Ford truck for my Uncle Fred's grocery store during summer vacations. The mother of the young but already famous Edna St. Vincent Millay was my favorite customer, even though her order was seldom more than the one package of yeast.

"Mrs. Millay wants her yeast," Uncle Fred would say, and I would go out and crank the Ford.

A tiny woman, she was fascinating to a youngster who had just discovered the pleasure of poetry—I was writing some pretty romantic stuff myself, from time to time.

She usually asked me in for milk and cookies, although sometimes she was too busy in her garden. But the times I sat in her kitchen were filled with her chatter and my tongue-tied silence. I was awed by the fact that she was the mother of Edna St. Vincent Millay, a graduate of Camden High School and currently a great success in Boston and New York, attracting hundreds to readings of her poems.

51

Her mother never mentioned her famous daughter, probably because she thought the young delivery boy was too young for such discussion. She did talk about things going on in Camden, however, like the sailing regatta that had just anchored in the harbor or her trouble in finding boys to pull the weeds in her flower gardens.

"If they don't pull every weed, they might just as well stay home," she would say, eyeing me closely to see if I might be converted to a weed-puller in time of emergency.

There were many visits with the Model-T during the summer and usually with just an order of yeast. But one trip stands out most vividly. I had completed my delivery and set the spark in just the right position to make an impressive departure. It was on a hill, and I didn't know the brake wasn't functioning. Never did a young driver have a wilder ride down a Maine-coast hill and with such good fortune as no obstructing vehicles.

A few days later, in the Camden library, I opened Edna St. Vincent Millay's first volume of poetry, *Renascence*. In the first few lines I read, "I turned and looked another way/and saw three islands in a bay." This poem—which started off so simply and which, before she was twenty, had launched her career as a major American poet—was not fully comprehended by the young reader. But it kindled a lifelong curiosity about poetry as a way of looking at things, in contrast to prose. In this instance, these were the same islands I saw every day, but I had never seen them in the context of the intense feeling of her highly personal identification of them with what was vital to her in life.

If there has been any consistency in my life, it has been the belief that poetry is one of the most important ingredients of a civilized society. Some would give priority to music, but I say poetry because it involves words as well as sound, and rationality as well as rhythm.

I think that experience in Camden opened my eyes to poetry as a way of looking at things—seeing common things differently, reporting common feelings differently. How did Sandburg look at Chicago? Whitman at America? Frost at his birches?

In the past decade, I believe, the younger generation of Americans has discovered poetry as its own form of communication. To be sure, there is Sandburg's guitar with most of it. But I look with pleasure these days at a generation that has found a way to express its frustrations, its hatred of war and its love of peace, its sense of values and its longing for simplicity. I hope these young folk singers increase—both they *and* their listeners. Theirs is the way of looking at things that is poetry. It may indeed help turn this world around—there are so many of them and the availability of audience is so large.

The other day I heard a recording, done many years ago, of Edna St. Vincent Millay reading her poetry. As much as I responded to her poetry again, I realized how overdramatic such performances were in the 1920s, and how isolated.

I go back to my discovery in Camden of poetry as a way of looking at things. I welcome its abundance and its naturalness in the present.

An Unusual Schoolhouse

I WAS SITTING in the rear of the canoe, with the boy in front of me casting dry-flies for landlocked salmon. It was early twilight on a lake in northern Maine, one of the most beautiful wilderness spots I have ever seen.

The sun had just slid behind the tallest spruce, and it was just the right time for the salmon or trout to start feeding. Naturally, the boy's attention was on his rod and the beautifully cast fly as it lighted on the blue gray water.

He was oblivious of my presence, except perhaps for some small resentment of it. However, it was my job to be there. I was being paid for it, as part of one of the strangest teaching assignments a person could have.

The boy was the 12-year-old son of the proprietor of the famous King and Bartlett Camps, situated straight into the Maine woods over a logging road from the nearest town. This was when summer people stayed put in one place for a month or two. Getting to this wilderness camp was hard enough to encourage the long stay. I never knew why most of them came from Philadelphia.

Because the fishing and hunting camp opened in the early spring and closed in the late fall, it was necessary for the proprietor's son to miss parts of the school year in his home city. I had been hired for the summer between my two earliest college years to be the son's tutor, so that he could keep up with his class on return to school.

My difficulty was keeping up with the son. Showing not the slightest interest in books or studying, and exceedingly active in all kinds of fishing that abounded in the streams and lakes around the wilderness camp, he was a reluctant pupil.

I think I learned more than he did that summer. It was my first experience with fly-fishing, and he not only knew the conventional flies but invented some.

You can imagine the problem that confronted me in pinning this kind of boy down long enough to get a little history, grammar, arithmetic, and civics into him.

I soon worked out a system. I told him I would swap his teaching me the art of fly-fishing for equal time for me to teach him what he needed. He would do this by taking time out on the trail and not having to hole up in a cabin for lessons. "I will go wherever you want to," I said, "just as long as you will spend some time working at what they will test you on back at school."

I probably was the "hikeingest" teacher ever. I walked miles that summer from stream to stream to lakes with my active pupil. I won't call him a student or scholar, which he wasn't — except with gun and rod.

I did expect him, of course, to do a little studying each evening, for review on the trails. His response was, fortunately, affirmatively enforced by his father, who wanted his money's worth from my presence at the camps.

The "school" itself, nevertheless, was in the canoes and the larger rowboats or walking the trails. Occasionally, it was in the old buckboard with which we went out to civilization to meet some incoming guests.

My knapsack full of books was the traveling desk. Questions and answers were tossed back and forth while on the go — mostly as we hiked, and there were miles of trails on which to do it. One thing he didn't like to do in a daily routine was sit still — except in a boat or next to our fire with freshly caught trout frying in the pan.

Because both my father and mother were teachers, I sought outlines and advice from them by mail — especially those basics to emphasize for his upcoming school test. It was primarily up to me to keep his friendship while everlastingly assaulting him with questions and explanations of the material on which we were working.

I learned a lot about fishing that summer. I never did know just what he learned about grammar and history. I do know he finished high school.

What did he do after that? He went back to his beloved lakes, free from teachers. The best fishermen are not always Ph.D.'s.

Like Peas in a Pod

FIFTY YEARS AGO, exactly, I was criss-crossing northern New England as a textbook salesman. From Aroostook County, Maine, to Chittendon County, Vt., was my territory. My conveyance was a Model-A Ford, and my customers were school superintendents and principals.

I don't think there were many towns and cities in that loosely populated area that I did not visit at least once in those two years. In the beginning there were a few schools that I walked around several times, as a wet-eared college graduate, before I got up enough courage to enter and make my pitch.

I lived "on the road" the first year, traveling almost every day; therefore I saw a lot of northern New England turf. My turf.

At that time, these three northern states bore little resemblance to each other. Each had characteristics that made it different. Maine, except in Aroostook County, always gave one the feeling of not being far from the Atlantic Ocean. New Hampshire was ruggedly reaching for the sky with its White Mountains. Vermont huddled against New York State, separated in part only by Lake Champlain. No sea breezes came from the lake.

The other day, fifty years and retirement later, I criss-crossed the three states on a two-day drive that covered some 700 miles. Thus I had the feeling of dropping down on all three states almost at the same moment, with no sense of borders as I drove from one to the other and back again.

This time, simply because I was concentrating on my surroundings rather than focusing on getting to some particular place, I found that many of the old differences have been wiped away by progress.

TV antennas march from rooftop to rooftop across the three

states. Each has its trailers and trailer parks as part of the general look-alike syndrome. Each has the same kind of facilities and trails for its skiers, giving all such mountains the same developed appearance.

Mr. McDonald and Colonel Sanders have invaded and conquered, raising their familiar flags beside the roads and highways clogged with traffic.

I could go on and on with the list of look-alikes that have smothered the old differences once enjoyed by each state of northern New England.

It might not be a bad idea for each to give up its sovereignty as a state, if the Indians will permit Maine to, and pack a bigger wallop in Washington as a large political bloc. Any one of the present three governors, each with his own personal style, would fit into the governor's chair of the state of New Vermainhamp. The people of the three states already have shown that they like a rugged individual as chief executive, probably a throwback to the years when each state housed its distinctive brand of ruggedly individualistic citizens.

Times have changed in fifty years and I have changed with them, probably no more for the better than have the three states during that period.

I have always said that I was born too late, having been born into the fading twilight of the 1890s just after the turn of the century. I am horse-and-carriage oriented. I like dirt roads. I get claustrophobia if I am long in a place without a lot of elbow room.

I am writing this in New Hampshire, waiting for my car's wheels to be aligned after a spring of pot-holes in the so-called hard-top roads. I would prefer to be waiting for my horse to be shod.

What this country needs is a good blacksmith to hammer some of the old virtues, like thrift, back into us. We look alike, as do our respective surroundings. But we don't act alike with regard to the basic principles that were a common bond in a less mobile nation.

As I said, the 1890s have always beckoned me, with their horse-and-carriage style and the pace of life that went with it. Maybe that's why, on the way to the auto-repair shop this morning, I found myself singing at the top of my voice that old 19th-century song "I'm Only a Bird in a Gilded Cage."

In earlier days, in 1928 to be specific, the driving pace and less-cluttered traffic made it possible for a would-be poet to compose lines while drifting through the countryside. My impression of part of New Hampshire, for instance, initiated this poem, written fifty years ago and popped out of an old file I was searching through the other day.

Challenge

Among the spruce-propped hills I drove one day
In January—hills of granite thrust
Against a granite sky to strike a dust
That fell as snow, yet gray, and all the way
I looked on shanties tumbled in decay.
Nor could I answer what intrinsic trust
First brought the settlers to these hills—what gust
of withered wind had whispered them to stay.

That night I listened to the bragging talk
Of tired men come down from hills to thaw
Before the tavern grate—and hard one mock
A Youngster's boast of skill with ax and saw . . .
"You call yourself a woodsman, son?" "H---, no!
But I can make a livin' at it, Joe!"

The Horse Was King

THERE ARE TWO HORSES in a long-empty pasture that I drive by every day. Two large and matched work horses, tan with black manes and tails, munch the green grass in a slow and stately fashion. I always slow down to watch them.

Horses, as a distinguished species of living things, do something to me. I identify with them. They were close to me in my earlier years; but even now, whenever they appear—in the distance, or pushing noses over a roadway fence for greener grass, at a horse show, a fair, or carrying a rider along a path or on a country road—they trigger excitement. It is like seeing a full moon rising over a lake and remembering that it was on such a night under the same moon you first kissed a girl.

Ben Betts, whom I have seen around horses for forty years, identifies closely with them. They are a necessary part of his experience of living. Dr. Albert Grass is, to be sure, a veterinarian, but when I see him around horses I know that he also identifies with them—not just as a doctor but as a person who responds to horses. So also is Bill Davisson, exhibiting his joy in a carriage behind a good horse. Sally Swift, Phoebe Chamberlin, and Kathy Emerson are, in the best sense of the word, "horsey" women. They glow in the presence of a horse—anywhere, any horse. You have to look closely, but if you, too, are "horsey" you catch the unspoken wave of mutual understanding that floats between human beings and horses.

Not a very large percentage of people these days identify with horses. Time was when almost everybody shared this relationship. It has to be experienced at a young age to get into the blood—as I was with my Shetland stallion, with my uncle's livery stable, with my father's leading the 4th of July parade in Castine on Black Mike, with the time we had horses here when the kids were young.

There was a period in history when the horse was king. Society depended on him, just as we depend on our automobiles today. It would have been difficult for many generations of people to live and to make a living without horses. The invention of the automobile quickened the pace of day-to-day life in America and swept horses into limbo. Now we cut our budgets thin to gather extra cash for the increasing burden of gasoline expense. There is nothing affordable, at least as far as I know, that appears likely to replace the automobile.

As for me, I'd pretty much settle for the return of the horse. We could use a slower pace and a breathing spell.

Was life really so bad in Brattleboro, Rutland, Barre, Portland, or Waterville when every person, every parcel, every plow depended on a horse to get places?

Well, we'll let that thought perish.

But I find myself with a yen, at times, to have been a part of that period in American life — especially the glorious horse-and-carriage period, from 1870 to 1910, roughly between the Civil War and World War I. It may be that because I grew up on the tail end of that period I am so fascinated by what I missed.

In its heyday, the kingdom of the horse was far from a dull one. The pace was slow, of course, and people knew little about the world outside their city or town. Most of the country depended on weekly newspapers for news, and they depended on themselves for entertainment. Those were days of innumerable picnics, of guitar and banjo clubs, country fairs, and traveling actors with their one-night shows.

There were times when it was a big event for five or six young couples to hire a buckboard from a livery stable and drive its two horses on an all-day trip to the next town, eighteen or so miles away. Then, after a night in its little hotel, it was an all-day trip home.

It was the horse — big and little horses, slow and fast

horses — that made it possible for people to go leisurely where we go so speedily today.

Uncle Warren finally closed his livery stable a few years after the automobile arrived. He put away his buffalo robes, stored his carriages, sold his horses.

"What are you going to do now, Warren?" he was asked.

"Putter around. People will go back to horses again, pretty soon," he said. "I'm leaving the sign up out front there — the one that says 'Hooper's Livery and Standing Stable.'"

When Style Was Neat Simplicity

ONE OF THE ESSENCES of life is style. I don't mean literary style or fashion style. My thoughts lead me to the definition of *style* as "construction in any art period, work, employment: as the Byzantine style or modern style." It is from the context of this definition in *Webster's* that I make the following comments.

As a kid in school up in Maine, or down in Maine (whichever way you want to look at it), I was always impressed with the style of the coaches used by British royalty and pictures of which adorned our history books. Some of those old relics still appear on TV when the queen opens a new government or on some similar occasion. They still have more style than the more recent traditional hats, wide and upturned, that the queen wears while sitting in the old royal coach. I always admired the coaches, even though I didn't have the slightest idea that they were built for the royal family by a family named Hooper.

So in 1932, when my wife and I were riding in the upper deck of one of the English buses in London's Piccadilly Circle and came face to face with the second-story sign reading "Hooper, By Appointment to Her Majesty the Queen," we left the bus immediately to investigate.

We were, indeed, in the London headquarters of the firm that had been making coaches for the royal family since time immemorial. They were delightful to talk with and presented us with a "History of Coachmaking," which we still prize. I might add right here that no amount of research by our daughter living in England has been able, even remotely, to connect our name with those historical coach makers — maybe seventeenth cousins twice removed!

I often wonder, however, if it were more than coincidence that my grandfather in Castine, Maine, was a carriage maker, specializing in buckboards for his own livery stable. And this may well be the time that I should confess that I have never seen an automobile with as much character and *style* as the carriages that preceded it. I'll give or take a little on the sleek styles of some of the modern cars. But on the whole, our forebears rode in some very stylish vehicles, whether drawn by an old nag or by a high-stepping Morgan.

Both you and I are aware of the beautiful carriages on exhibit at the Shelburne Museum in Vermont. Some of them were "hunkies," but some of them had a style no automobile has been able to duplicate. I have seen them in livery stables in Maine, New Hampshire, and Vermont during the few years I was able to see livery stables before they became obsolete.

I have especially seen them in the old catalogs of the Concord Coach manufacturers, and more particularly in the Brockway catalog of 1906, one of my favorite possessions — the catalog of Wm. Brockway Estate of Homer, N.Y., a firm that started making high-grade carriages in 1851.

I like, as a foreword to the display of their craftsmanship, the statement of George A. Brockway, manager in 1906, who wrote:

"The vehicles illustrated in the following pages are the latest and most approved styles for this season, and the standard of workmanship and general makeup of Brockway carriages will be maintained and improved. This old house, established in 1851, will be in a position to supply your wants promptly and the quality will be of the highest grade."

No Chevrolet engines substituted for Oldsmobile engines in cars that were bought by prideful Oldsmobile admirers. Just guaranteed Brockway carriages! And just listen to some of the guaranteed craftsmanship: Surrey with a 1¼-inch Cushion Tire, or Cut-Under Standhope, Victoria Top, or Park Runabout with 1½-inch Cushion Tire, or a real serviceable vehicle, the Business Concord with Wheels for City Use.

What I mean is that *style* in vehicles didn't originate with the American-made Thunderbird or the imported Porsche, on big tires and throbbing with power.

Style has been with us since the royal coaches, through the years with the Concord and Brockway carriages, and up to the present dilemma of what automobile manufacturers are going to design on their drawing boards to meet the fancy of the public and the fragility of its pocketbook. It will have to have something up front, but with a carburetor as parsimonious as a Calvin Coolidge.

For several hundred years the style of the carriages was taken for granted, with an emphasis on simplicity and the use for which it was designed. If there were any extravagance involved, it was the quality of the horse that was hitched to it.

The difference today is to what extent the size of the vehicle can be in relation to the amount of gas-eating horsepower attached to it. Maybe this indulgence of the public's obsession with size, and resulting dilemma for designers, can continue for awhile.

But, maybe again, the public will once more discover that there is style in simplicity—not only in vehicles but in a way of life.

Saluting the Schoolhouse

I AM STANDING in front of a schoolhouse, tipping my hat. I am tipping my hat *to* the schoolhouse, to its red brick front, to its windows with pupils' drawings pasted to them, to its large oak door. And in giving this salute to a building, I am paying a tribute to what I think is the essence of this country's particular character.

America's unique system of public education is the basic mixing bowl for its people of all colors, of all degrees of economic condition, of people constitutionally free to utilize their differences as well as their common bond as citizens of a free country.

I cannot visualize a United States of America, as we know this nation, without its system of locally controlled public schools. Certain nations have symbols by which people associate them with their historic image, something that speaks of the character of that nation. France has its Arc de Triomphe and England its Tower of London. But America can point with pride to its public schoolhouse — one in every city and town and in many of its remote villages.

No other nation has built into its political and social patterns a philosophy of freedom and representative government as dependent on access to free education as has the United States, almost from its beginning. Here the future voters learn to read and write, to figure and find their relation to the history that has preceded them, to create, to play, to work.

Here, in the schoolhouses, was planted man's ability to get to the moon and at the same time to develop the most enlightened civil rights legislation anywhere on earth.

It was in the public schoolhouse that were nurtured the basic ingredients of this nation's industrial development and, at the same time, its capacity for concern that its environment shall be balanced with this industrial growth. It was in the schoolhouse, primarily the public schoolhouse, that America learned how to be America.

As I look back over public education, I see the last hundred years of it closely — through my father's and mother's experiences as teachers from the early 1890s and through my own experience. I was never a teacher, but turned to writing and newspaper work. I did, however, peddle textbooks for five years, visiting most of the schoolhouses in northern New England and all the public schools in New York City. I am biased, probably, in my regard for the public schoolhouse as an American institution because I have been in so many of them. Give me credit for my bias, also, for having served on a local school board, a state board, and the New England Board of Higher Education.

I can smell the Dustbane-cleaned floors of the old schoolhouses every time I pass a school today.

When my mother started teaching in her first schoolhouse on Marshall's Island, off the Maine coast eighty-nine years ago and at the age of sixteen, teaching was hardly a profession, but it was an honorable vocation. And when later she had received her diploma as a teacher from the Eastern State Normal School at Castine, she felt that she was entering a noble career, as did my father.

In later years, as my brother and I were growing up, we felt there was something important about what our father and mother were doing, teaching in schoolhouses.

Father, as principal of a grammar school, and mother, principal of an elementary school, brought the institution of public education into our home in much the same way that families used to place the Bible on the parlor table.

As I say, I may be biased. But when you are thinking about things that have given this country its elements of greatness, don't forget the public schoolhouses.

New England Boiled Dinner

NOT MANY HOUSEHOLD COOKS put a New England boiled dinner together these days. I don't know when it started to lose its popularity as a special New England meal, but today it can be counted among the antiques.

A New England boiled dinner was not fast food. It was an event, requiring considerable preparation. There came a time, obviously, when cooks chose to avoid the effort. The multiple increase of foods and recipes over the years put this meat-and-vegetable dish on the back shelf.

So why do the people of my generation still look upon this dish fondly? Because it tasted good, and still does when somebody else cooks it. There are a few restaurants that occasionally still do serve it.

Its ingredients are simple — corned beef and six vegetables, boiled in the same pot. The vegetables must be obtained and prepared for cooking are turnips, cabbage, carrots, onions, beets, and small potatoes with the skin on. A good cook knows when to add each of them to the boiling pot. They aren't all dropped in at the same time, for their cooking requirements vary.

The beef, a special brisket cut from the breast of the critter, must be corned over a period of several days before it is even ready for the pot. Mother would hand me a long fork and ask me to go down the cellar "to turn the beef." I would take the cover off a large crock and poke down into the solution of water, salt, sugar, and saltpeter and give the beef a turn. To be properly corned, the meat had to be turned once a day for four days.

Thus the New England boiled dinner, comprising these simple basic products, was not just a meal but an occasion. It was not served often, perhaps only several times a year. But for those who grew up with it, there lingers the desire to smell and taste it again.

There lingers also some of the special family occasions that seemed to be built around this particular meal. We never went for a visit to Uncle Fred's up in Camden without knowing that we would eat one of his New England boiled dinners. He would cut his own brisket down at his market, corn it in his own special concoction, and serve it with an air of majesty.

My brother and I, during our summers at Castine, were invited each year by Aunt Jen for a meal at her house. It was always a New England boiled dinner.

Both Camden and Castine were Maine-coast fishing towns. But when a special occasion demanded a choice meal, Uncle Fred and Aunt Jen went to the corning crock and the vegetable bin to create something rare and different.

One of the bonuses of a New England boiled dinner was that the leftovers could be ground up and served as red flannel hash, quite as tasty as the dinner and embellished with a simmering dropped egg on each serving.

Recently, my wife and I again pleasantly enjoyed both of these dishes. The hash, cooked by Dick Hamilton, was among the foods served by the ladies of Marlboro to spectators at Bill Davisson's harness-horse trail races. A woman from California, admired the corned beef hash, asked what vegetables were in it. They were being named when a head poked between the two to name a vegetable that had been missed. "And turnip," she said.

Last night we drove fifteen miles up the road to Hogback Mountain's Skyline Restaurant. Once a week, for a few weeks, it is serving New England boiled dinners. It was the real thing— corned beef surrounded by its six vegetables. Marion and I looked around among the people who had ordered this dish. Not many, if any, were under seventy years old.

The New England boiled dinner is still struggling along, a happy meal for some, but it deserves some new recruits.

Art of Debating

CHARLIE GUPTIL AND I had met at Bates. He had the kind of quick mind and ability to think on his feet that are basic requirements of a good debater. I was on the debating squad of which he was one of the leading members.

The next time we met, after college, was at the *Portland Press Herald,* where Guptil was a reporter and a stringer for the Associated Press. I was on the road as a textbook salesman and planned to hit Portland on Friday nights for an evening with Charlie. I was fascinated with the atmosphere of a newsroom, the clacking of the teletypes bringing the news of the world, the rhythm of typewriters pounding out the local and state news. In those times, the late '20s, there were several green visors among the newsmen. And there was city editor Red Cousins, a man of broad humor.

One of Charlie's beats was a nightly tour of the city in the police department's Black Maria. I made sure I had a ride, too.

The officer driving the Black Maria had the routine job of picking up drunks by covering the locations where they were most likely to be. We'd have a half a dozen ready to sleep it off in the city jail.

Once having taken care of this job, the Black Maria would make a wider sweep of the city, keeping an eye out for any unusual activity. I remember Portland in those days as a very dark city by night. There was a great contrast with its present brilliance.

Charlie Guptil went on from the *Press Herald* to a career abroad with the Associated Press.

He had two notable assignments — in Mexico City and in Rome. When I became an editor in Vermont, I was seeing Charlie Guptil's byline coming through the teletype and by mail nearly every day.

There are different opinions as to the best preparation for a newspaper career. Some place emphasis on a school of journalism. Others believe in a liberal arts course, including history and economics. Either generality may be right.

I wonder, however, if there is not another factor that at least helps, especially for newsmen who gravitate to the journalistic specialty, editorial writing.

You recall that Guptil was a debater. He was trained to develop a subject logically. He was trained to come to the point and weed out unnecessary words. He became skilled in writing tightly, to present his case with the same discipline that editorial writing requires.

If Charlie were the only debater to have gone into news-papering, I would hesitate to give credit to debating. But Ralph Blagdon, a high school classmate of mine, debated both in high school and college, and he became the editor of the *Boston Transcript.* Later he was editor of a New Hampshire newspaper, and his editorials had considerable impact on the politics of that state.

Further, Irwin Canham, who led a Bates debating team to England, was an active debater both in our high school and college. In his case, not only did he distinguish himself as chief editorial writer for the *Christian Science Monitor* but easily made the transfer to TV. There, his sharp commentaries have all the earmarks of a debater's logic.

Although my own affiliation with newsprint was delayed a few years by bookselling, I am sure that those Friday nights at the *Portland Press Herald* helped create my desire to get into news-papering. Charlie Guptil's enthusiasm in the Black Maria on dark Portland streets certainly helped as well.

Frost and Snow

INAUGURATION DAY for John F. Kennedy was cold and blustery. It was a day of hope for millions of Americans whose eyes were glued to their TV sets reflecting a vigorous young president calling for action and a renewal of spirit.

As long as there are people to remember that scene, however, there will always be the image of an old man participating in that ceremony. He was the poet Robert Frost, who had been asked by Kennedy to create and read a poem for the occasion.

There he stood, white hair blowing in the wind, his hands grasping the fluttering sheets of his poem, his words ringing out over the assembled dignitaries and huge audience in a

New England twang that came deep from the roots of America. From this distance in time, the image never seems to lose its strength—nor does the paradox of the wise old man in the midst of a scene in which the emphasis was on youth.

"Birches" and "Stopping by Woods on a Snowy Evening" are probably the poems by which Frost is best known, because of their constant inclusion in school anthologies. He was personally known, however, to the thousands of students in colleges where he was "poet in residence" and to the thousands who attended his readings over the years.

He is now dead, and the question of whether he was among the greatest of American poets is debated by critics; that exists even in Frost's official biography, written by Lawrance Thompson and published after the poet had died (as Frost had stipulated when he selected Thompson as his official biographer in 1939).

It was just fifty years ago I first met Robert Frost, which happened to be the occasion in front of the same blazing fireplace that Lawrance Thompson first met him. Thompson and I were classmates at Wesleyan University in Middletown, Conn. On that January night we were part of a small group of students invited by Prof. Wilbert Snow to spend an evening with Robert Frost at Snow's country farmhouse, several miles from the campus.

The group, as I recall, was confined to the staff of the college's literary magazine—very raw young writers of poetry and prose but wedded to the effort to produce a part of oneself in writing. With some young men and women this is a creative compulsion—just as striving for other forms of personal expression is a compulsion with others. Thus the chance to spend an evening with Frost was filled with excitement.

Who was Wilbert Snow, our host? He was a poet—poetry of the Maine coast, where he grew up. He was our favorite professor in the field of literature. Tall, lean, with a curved beak of a nose through which he seemed to speak, he was also a nonconformist among professors of those days. He didn't believe in giving grades, which got him into barrels of trouble with the academic bureaucrats.

He was also a politician of sorts, flaunting his being the lone Democrat on a faculty largely committed to the Republican cause. In fact, his participation in local Democratic affairs eventually led to his election as the lieutenant governor of Connecticut and a short interim as its governor, filling out an unexpired term.

Be that as it may, on that cold winter's night fifty years ago he was our host, as well as having as his guest for the weekend his friend Robert Frost. We had left our dormitories and gathered for the hike to Snow's farm. It was the kind of cold snow on the ground that squeaks at each footstep.

Inside, the stocky Frost, whose wide brow seemed to exude wisdom, stood in front of the fireplace warming his back and giving warm greetings to the young admirers as they threw off their heavy clothing and squatted on the floor.

The leaner and younger poet, Snow, was busy gathering firewood and seeing that everybody was comfortable. The talk went on until midnight, and ended with cider and doughnuts.

It ended? Not for Larry Thompson, it didn't. For him it was a beginning, at first a pursuit on his part to keep in touch with Frost and in 1939 the acceptance of him by Frost as the biographer who would spend many hours over many years with the poet in preparation for this task. This Larry did during the years after he had become a member of the English department at Princeton. After the years in which Frost was to win four Pulitzer Prizes, Larry also was to win one for volume two of the biography; the third and final volume was completed by an assistant from notes left by Thompson at the time of his own death.

Wilbert Snow died this year at the age of 93.

Some experiences remain indelibly imprinted in one's inner self. That evening with Frost and Snow was not only such an experience for me, but by coincidence was one in which a bit of American literary history took place and one that has never been told before — how, where, and when Robert Frost and his eventual biographer, Lawrance Thompson, first met and talked with each other.

Any News Today?

THE HEARTBEAT of a newspaper of forty-five years ago was in the column marked "Personals." This was the column, literally extending at times into two columns from top to bottom of an inside page, in which the activities of people as people were reported. It had nothing to do with public events or affairs. It was about people — the people of the newspaper's community.

It recorded their comings and goings, their guests and their anniversaries, the visits of their children coming home and the family get-togethers when cousins and aunts joined grandparents around the family board. It was personal as all get out, and that is why it was the best-read part of the newspaper.

How did you know what your neighbors were up to in Lubec or Rockland, Maine, if you didn't see it in the weekly newspaper's "Personals" column?

How did you know in Berlin or Keene, N.H., or in Barre or Brattleboro, Vt.? The first thing you turned to forty-five years ago was the "Personals" column.

What has happened to it? First, what has happened is the slow closing of society — from an open society of forty-five years ago to a closed one now in which nobody wants anybody to know when he is going away and leaving a house vacant.

You have seen the recent reports: "House vandalized while owners away." Or you have seen, "TV and Hi-Fi sets, estimated by police to be valued at $400, were stolen from the J. Smith house while the owners were in Florida."

Isn't it difficult, therefore, to realize that as late as thirty-five years ago people were not at all reluctant to tell the newspaper when they were leaving on a trip?

Let's take a specific example of the kind of "Personals" reporting that most newspapers did less than half a century ago. And let us not forget that people not only were glad to give this kind of news but also anxious to read about the other people in their area. This was the nitty-gritty news of small-town dailies and weeklies.

So, here we have Mrs. Grace Doak sitting at her desk in 1913 at the *Brattleboro Daily Reformer*. Her title was "Personal Reporter." Two afternoons a week she would take the trolley car to West Brattleboro — talking with people on the car, calling at the general store, visiting a few homes where she knew there were people who had their ears to the ground on neighbor's news. On other days she would hang around the railroad station.

Her easy approach to people was, "What do you know today?" They knew she meant what news did they know. . . .

As the years went on, she pinpointed people she could call by phone. "What do you know today?"

Daily for thirty years she went from store to store on Main Street, talking with the clerks, the proprietors, and any acquaintances she spotted. "What do you know today? Any news?"

She would come up with people planning trips, having guests, even who was going to have Sunday dinner with whom, until we had to set a limit of "no visit is news unless it takes place at least fifty miles away."

Grace Doak, thick-skinned, friendly, inquisitive, and with an arched nose for news. "Personals," a part of a newspaper in an open society. They permeated the newspapers of New England. They were what really sold newspapers.

You miss them, if you are among the older readers. More than likely, you've never heard of them if you are among the younger. They are no longer possible as a form of news. No more "Personal" news of the comings and goings of the people in your community. Why? Society lost its respect for the rights and safety of its neighbors. It substituted robbery, larceny, and vandalism.

Any solution?

In the meantime, the reporters such as Grace Doak, who retired in 1942 because nobody had her kind of news any longer, have given way to reporters of OPEC and the "Nuclear Syndrome."

A Night Watchman's Reward

I NEVER THOUGHT much about it before, but how did I come to be a night watchman in a hotel at the age of 21? What was I watching for?

Well, it was a happy coincidence. I had been fired at the Oak Bluffs Hotel on Martha's Vineyard because I couldn't take the guff of the proprietor nor could he take mine. I was his printer of menus and writer of the in-house newsletter. The firing was an abrupt affair. I was on the island and suddenly without a job. This was in the summer of 1925.

So I hitchhiked down to the other end of the island to Edgartown and applied for a job at the Colonial Inn.

"Want to be a night watchman? We just fired one."

"Sure."

I was given a room in the attic and draped with a contraption from which I could fit a key into boxes on each of the three floors to indicate I had been fire-watching there every hour during the night.

The original inn has since burned down.

I was naive. I didn't know what went on during the nights in hotels. I got an education.

However, I shall not dwell on that side of my education as much as on what happened each morning when I went off duty at 7:00 A.M., or shortly thereafter.

Edgartown had a lovely beach—long and white and deep. I went to the beach each morning for a swim before sleeping into the day.

I soon discovered that the only other person on the beach at that hour was a beautiful woman—raven-black hair and a white bathing suit. We never spoke; I just looked.

I learned that this ravishing beauty was a poet named Michael Strange, no less feminine for the first name.

She was, or had been, or was about to be the wife of John Barrymore, the Great Profile of our silent movies.

I simply knew that I would lie on the white beach after a night of punching clocks in the Colonial Inn and marvel each morning at what I saw on the edge of the ocean.

Of course, I had never seen Jackie Kennedy at that time, but my memory cannot separate her from Michael Strange. It surprised me as to how white a bathing suit could become when attached to a sun-bronzed skin that met the morning each day.

I can't recall Michael Strange ever speaking to me, even though she was staying at the Colonial Inn at the time. Lord knows, I didn't have the courage to speak to her.

All of this came back as I read a review in the *New York Times* of a biography of John Barrymore, in which one of his wives was listed as Michael Strange.

It rang a bell. She was the beautiful phenomenon who came dashing out of the waves each morning at Edgartown as I lay with one eye open to watch.

It became a ritual with me. I punched the clocks all night long with the hope of a sunny morning. I helped drunks to bed, with the hope of a sunny morning. I showed transient guests the elevators at 4:00 A.M., with the hope of a sunny morning. And if the sun shone, I was rewarded.

If the sun did not shine I was just another night watchman who had gone to bed after a hurried breakfast, to wake up in the afternoon for another day, or night, of hope.

Michael Strange was a poet — yet I can't remember reading one line of what she wrote. I must, someday.

The review of the Barrymore biography reminded me of the poetic lines Michael Strange possessed naturally, without writing a word. As long as I live, she will remain a mermaid, whether John Barrymore knows that was what he married or not.

She was part of a young man's sunrise, some fifty years ago.

The Last Ride

THE TIME HAD COME for me and my pony, Xavier, to go our separate ways. At eighteen, I no longer rode him because I was too large. We had found a buyer, after shopping around for a new owner who would give him a good home. Xavier was also eighteen at that time, an age when he would need a comfortable retirement.

We harnessed Xavier to the two-wheel wicker-sided cart and started the last ride to his new owner, a man with several small children. My brother had volunteered to ride with me. His interest was bicycles, but he realized what my pony had meant to me. It was a ten-mile ride to his new home.

I thought of the hours and the years I had spent with Xavier. Every day for six years I had walked the quarter mile, in all kinds of weather, to the stable where he was given free lodging. This meant twice a day for feeding. During my morning and afternoon newspaper routes his feeding coincided with riding him from the route back to the stable. This I took in stride, merely lengthening my stride in the morning to make sure that I got to school on time.

It was my impression that in those times, sixty-odd years ago, there were more boys owning ponies or horses than girls. My observation of the present indicates that the opposite is true. Anyhow, we had a pony club in which there were more boys than girls. From cowboys and Indians in the woods and hills back of my home to rides in the countryside with a packed lunch, we kept our ponies active on weekends.

While Xavier was naturally a pert and attractive pony, he was a mess in the winter with his long winter coat of hair. He took plenty of brushing and currying to make him presentable. I never begrudged the time spent doing this. Xavier and I were close.

Fortunately, the horse shows and state fairs were in seasons when he was a glossy black, dappled in the sunlight. These were times when results were possible from the time spent in his stall, brushing and wiping his muscular body. The blue ribbons he won far outnumbered the red. It was only recently that I came upon the stack of ribbons, disintegrated over the years.

Of course, there were some show classes in which each pony was judged under halter. This seemed the fairest to the pony. When judged in his cart there was another factor between the pony and the judge's eye — the cart and harness. The harness needed to be pretty shiny, and this was where an older harness could detract from the pony's overall points. I was glad Xavier could earn what he did on his own merit.

As we were driving along on the last ride, for us, I was thinking of how many times my mother and father had driven him in a sleigh to the evening school where they taught English to foreign-speaking adults. Xavier spent the evening tied up beside the boiler in the basement.

I thought of how rarely he had been frightened enough to run away, the most notable time being when a team of runaway horses came up behind us and Xavier bolted. He kept ahead of the runaway team for a quarter of a mile, just far enough to reach a steep hill that slowed the horses behind us.

Today, I can feel the smooth skin in the show ring, and I can see his ears come forward as I talked to him. I can smell with pleasure the aroma of a pony lathered up from a good gallop.

My brother and I approached Xavier's new home. I had walked him most of the way, to delay the parting.

We took the trolley back to Auburn. It was a quiet ride. There wasn't much to talk about.

How It Began

WHEN WE BOUGHT this place nearly forty years ago it was so dilapidated that some of our friends threatened to burn it down as a favor. Since the suggestion was made just before the Fourth of July we stayed here that night to be sure that it was no more than a suggestion.

To be sure, we knew that we would practically have to rebuild the house, but we wanted to keep as much of the old structure as possible, to utilize its old beams and to follow its general lines that fitted into the hillside. We had our ideas of how we wanted to build and to remodel. A young architect, whose office was in the same building as our Stephen Daye Press, whipped the ideas into blueprints. This was back in the Great Depression, and contractors were hungry. It would be sheer folly to try to do today what we were able to do then in doing over an old house.

The previous occupants of the house were two elderly brothers who eked out an existence from the land, a few chickens, and a couple of cows. It had made little difference to them that water from the hills above ran through the cellar every spring or that the wind whistled through the cracks in winter. They holed up in the kitchen and let the rest of the house fill up with cans and rubbish.

I had first seen the place when I ran out of worms fishing in the brook that flows along the road down below the house. The old men let me dig some next to the chicken yard. I made a mental note of their age and figured that it would not be long before the farm would be for sale. It had struck my fancy as the kind of rural setting we were looking for—not too far from town, and isolated from other houses.

One evening a doctor friend and his wife arrived late for dinner at the house we were then renting. He explained his delay by saying he had just been called to a small farm where one of two older brothers passed away during the emergency visit. The surviving brother had told him the farm would have to be sold.

It was the place where I had dug my worms. I soon learned who the executor was, a man whose sharp business dealings were far too keen for my wanting to deal with him directly. I needed help.

I remembered a horse trader in a nearby town for whom I had done a favor. Actually, I had only written a letter to a judge praising the character of the man, who was allegedly operating a still at his remote home on a back road. The judge had given him the opportunity to present letters on his behalf, and as I had known him as a responsible horse trader I was glad to oblige. He, in turn, had said he hoped sometime he could return the favor. I called him up and asked him to drop by the office when in town. I told him I needed help.

He came. I explained about the smart executor whom I wanted him to meet and to outtrade on a house and ten acres. I was sure, I said, it would take a horse trader of his long experience to accomplish the mission.

His eyes lit up—he was eager. So I gave him a check comprising our savings and told him to get the deed in his name and then immediately transfer it to us.

As he left the office he turned and waved the check. "See you in San Francisco," he said. I must admit that at this point I did begin to have some qualms about the whole thing.

In a few hours he was back with the papers ready for my signature. We had bought the house, barn, and ten acres at what was certainly the right price, because the small amount I had given him was enough.

This was the scant beginning of what has been our home for almost forty years. It was a time for starting to plan, to give free rein to the kind of house in which we wanted to live, to see an old house retain its identity and yet lend itself to the structural requirements necessary for many more years of usefulness. It was the beginning of our long devotion to this land, this home, which are so much a part of us today.

Cleaning Up the Barn

JIM, A BOY from down the road, was helping me tidy up the barn. The idea was to throw as much of the stuff away as possible, so that anybody could move around without knocking something over.

He stood in the doorway and looked around. "Where do we begin?" he asked.

"That's what I've been wondering for years, ever since the animals left these stalls empty," I said.

Jim opened the door of a box-stall and disappeared from sight. He emerged with a large rusty bait box filled with tangled lines, tins of wet and dry flies, and rusty reels.

"Want me to throw this in the barrel?"

"No, you better put that on a shelf in the grain room, and I'll untangle it sometime."

Jim's eyes turned to a short pair of skis with rollers on them.

"You don't use these any more, do you?" he asked.

"I don't," I said, "but every kid that comes around does. Those are grass skis. Kids take them up the path to the meadow and have a ball riding them right back down to the barn. Can't throw those away."

"Well, shall we start with all the boards," Jim asked, as he picked up a varnished three-foot board with which to start his pile of loose lumber.

"If you do it with that board, the grandchildren will chase you all the way to West Brattleboro. Do you know what a Bongo Board is?"

I then explained to him how one can become lost in frustration trying to balance a Bongo Board by standing on the board, feet apart on each side of the middle; then keeping the board from touching the floor while moving it along the roller, what a joy it is to hold it in even balance until the feet and body weight are in just the right positions.

"You can put that anywhere. The kids will always find it," I suggested.

By this time, Jim had decided I didn't want to throw anything away. But he stumbled onto the old Franklin stove that had been leaning against the south wall for some forty years.

82

"Going to get it fixed or throw it away?" he asked through the hair falling over his face.

"Well, neither," I said. "It can't be fixed, because part of the back is missing. And it is one of the first things my wife and I owned after we were married. Let it be."

We proceeded to move some old windows and screens into straight rows. We folded and neatly piled three old tents. Three lawn mowers, each with its limitations, were put in a neat line against the west wall. More and more room was opening up to walk in.

Since we could walk, we did. A path was now open to the north corner. Two battered brown knapsacks hung from a rafter. There were three until a year ago. At that time our daughter needed one more sack into which to put a small over-load for her trip home to England. She spotted her schooldays' knapsack. This she could carry over her shoulders.

At Bradley Airport, on her way home, Mary Ann's sack fell from her shoulders to the floor. The leather strap, rotten with age, had parted. We cadged some string from the information booth and tied the straps together just in time for her to make the plane.

So, while Jim and I were cleaning the barn, I said we better not throw the remaining two knapsacks away.

"You can never tell when someone might need one," I said.

"Looks pretty seedy," said Jim.

"Yes, they do, but you usually can find some string if they need it."

We were down to trunks, chests, and other low objects that had been concealed. Jim moved a trunk. Two mice skittered across the floor.

"Who says we don't have animals in the barn," Jim shouted.

He leaned over to lift the lid of an old trunk, but it didn't lift. It just came up off the floor, as though there were nothing in it.

Finally, the lid popped up. There, alone on the bottom, was a fox-fur neckpiece, the kind that a dressy lady years ago would have tossed around her neck to add style to her gown. I don't know where it came from. It was an old trunk—Aunt Marion's, I believe. Anyhow, it looked real sharp around Jim's neck.

"We haven't thrown much away," said Jim, as he put the fur piece back in the trunk.

"Doesn't seem so," I said. "I guess a barn without animals is just a good place to keep things."

The broken sleds, frayed tennis rackets, and ancient skis all nodded their heads—as Jim and I closed the barn door on a job well done.

"It Ain't Hay"

WHEN I AM DRIVING through farm country and see a farmer seated on his tractor in a distant field, I wonder what his thoughts are. What is he thinking about, all alone in his well-cultivated field? What filters through his mind as he looks ahead at the brown earth?

Certainly, the surroundings of the lone figure on a tractor could well be conducive to poetry. The rhythm of the straight row on row of plowed earth, rising and falling in the undulating field, could be something on which poetry is woven. The steady roar of the tractor engine forces a man into himself.

Is he creating something within himself, as well as with the plow? Or is he estimating his net profit, come harvest time? He may be concentrating only on whether his present pickup truck should be traded in for a new one.

I never know, of course, what these farmers are thinking. I do know there is something idyllic and dramatic in the picture of the farmer, alone with his tractor on soil that is being prepared for its crop.

There is a picture that always stands out in my mind since I read an old book on farming some years ago. The *Farmer's Companion,* published in 1834, devotes a number of pages to the challenging, productive, and independent life of a farmer. It argues this point in several ways. The one I like concerns a farmer standing on the manure in a cart being hauled across the field. "He stands with legs apart and flings the dung with an air of majesty."

I probably am attracted by these lone men on tractors because of my own addiction for their kind of machine. My own tractor is halfway between a riding lawn mower and the large farm tractor. With this I mow about an acre of lawn, plow snow in the winter, and haul whatever has to be hauled around the place. It is not a toy, as I found out after using it for several years. I had forgotten that I had taken the snow blower off and had not attached the mower. This made the rig top heavy with its tall, steel cab. Consequently, when I was riding it up to the barn, on a sidehill, it suddenly tipped over. I was fortunate not to be seriously hurt, and especially lucky there was no ledge or stone to shatter the glass beside me. It taught me to have greater respect for the idiosyncrasies of this piece of machinery. I can see better how the farm tractors get into danger spots, as they do.

As I am riding through the meadow, cutting to lawn length some of the grass we used to mow for hay, I am alone on a tractor with my own thoughts. The sound of the tractor has pushed me inward—somewhere between daydreaming and thinking. The children who used to play here have grown up. Their growing years provided a different perspective from that on this hot day of lawn mowing.

The meadow looked different in those earlier years, as does

the whole place. There were horses in the barn, and for those who would ride, the whole meadow would be turned into hay for the horses. This became a family affair, with an old McCormick mower hauled by the jeep. The jeep, plus a homemade hay platform on two wheels, moved from meadow to barn like a gliding haystack with no visible means of moving by itself.

An essential linking of man and grass is missing when no longer is there need or pleasure of turning the meadow into windrows of hay to be stowed in the vast haymow of this now empty barn. Perhaps as one grows older, one becomes neater. He expects life to be a little more orderly. He trims his inner habits a little more closely. His outer habits take lawns and their trimmings as a matter of course.

There is no laughter in the meadow, only the echo of it as the tractor follows its cutting pattern. There is a kind of contentment from the reveries that accompany this present chore.

My Day with Eleanor

MY IMAGE OF President Franklin D. Roosevelt is the news photo of him seated between Churchill and Stalin at Yalta. I see Roosevelt today, as I saw him in that picture, enshrouded in his large, dark cape.

In a similar fashion, I remember my visit to Campobello Island when it was enshrouded in a large, dark cape of fog. This was in the 1930s, and I was visiting Johnny Johnston, son of the man in charge of maintenance of this Roosevelt estate on Campobello Island.

Johnny was teacher-coach at Brattleboro High School. My companion on the trek to Campobello was Sam Lincoln, sales manager for our Stephen Daye Press. It was an unconscionable distance from Vermont to Campobello, which was just off

Eastport, Maine, and especially so in a Model A Ford. We took turns keeping awake and driving.

Johnny met us in Eastport, and his little lobster boat had a struggle getting through the rushing tide in the narrow reach between Campobello and Eastport. The warmth of the Johnston family wiped away our weariness. Naturally, our conversation with Mr. Johnston turned to his relations with the Roosevelt family and the responsibilities of his job.

He described Mrs. Roosevelt as an exceedingly friendly person, who treated the Johnston family as though they were members of her own. Her demands for attention to her house were few, and Mr. Johnston attributed this to his efforts to anticipate any requests she might have and to take care of them ahead of her visit.

Our own meeting with Mrs. Roosevelt didn't come until the day after our arrival. It was a rainy day, and the daytime lowering fog made the island seem bare, which it nearly was. The Johnston's house and the large Roosevelt cottage loomed out of the fog only when we were a few feet from them. Shortly after noon we went to the cottage to make a call on Mrs. Roosevelt, who was spending a few days there.

The screen door was unlatched, and we slipped inside and said "hello."

Then we said "hello" a little louder, but there was no answer in the room, made dark by the outside drizzle. After all, it was a very large cottage — thirty-two rooms, eighteen bedrooms. Shortly after that we drifted down to the small boat landing.

We could hear oars, on a rowboat coming along the shore. When it arrived at the dock, a tall, angular Eleanor Roosevelt, in rain clothes, stepped from the boat to the dock. With her were son James and a male visitor. She called to Johnny to walk along with her to her cottage. This gave him the opportunity to introduce Sam and me. She wanted to know where we

87

lived and were we relatives of Johnny. For whatever other kind of communication she might have been known for, on that island on that foggy day, she was a master of small talk.

After a half-hour at her cottage having a cup of tea, we returned to the Johnston home. We hardly felt we had been conversing with the First Lady. She seemed almost to be a native of that rugged island.

It was not until a dozen years later that I met Mrs. Roosevelt again. It was at a party at the Waldorf Towers, given by the U.S. delegation to the United Nations, that I could thank her again for the tea at Campobello. She was dressed in a gray tweed suit and was animated and popular with the guests.

I said then that it was a mystery how anybody as homely as Eleanor Roosevelt could be so impressive.

Recently I read a newspaper story of what has happened to Campobello in recent years. The island is connected to Eastport by a bridge. The Roosevelt cottage is jointly operated by Canada and the United States as a memorial. Last year 140,000 visitors walked through the cottage. It has a year-round staff.

I can only contrast this with my memory of my visit to Campobello, some forty years ago. For myself, I prefer to see the present memorial as the same image I have: the big house sitting under its cape of fog, occupied by the friendly woman who served us tea.

Distractions

WORKING HERE AT my stand-up desk, I find my conversation being splintered by those distracting chickadees coming and going to and from the bird feeder. They are only a few feet away from the window. What catches my eye, no matter how much I try to bend it toward the paper, is the peculiarity with which chickadees come and go. They are swoopers — a few feet in a straight line, then a drop of a foot or two until the swoop brings them back to the straight line. Perhaps I should call them "Hooper's swoopers."

Their great numbers make it hard to keep from watching. Maybe I have a secret desire to see one run out of steam on his swoop and fall to the ground. One never has.

Being distracted as I am at the moment, I have started mulling over the kinds of things that distract me. They add up, come to think of it.

For instance, while the chickadees are in abundance there is a dearth of nuthatches coming to our feeder, so far this winter, except one lone fellow. The minute he shows up I drop everything and scan the bushes, the ground, and the feeder for another nuthatch. Thus far there hasn't been another, and so the distraction continues every time the lone one shows up.

A similar distraction in the same area and from this same desk is the frequent appearance of a mole or a mouse, which darts into sight for an instant and then back to cover. I still don't know which it is, and I guess what keeps me curious is the hope it is not a small rat.

Anyhow, it is distracting — as is the sound of the oil burner coming on at a time when the wood furnace supposedly is giving enough heat not to make the thermostat signal the oil burner. This calls for investigation, completely putting aside what I was writing.

I put my wood-scarred hands into tough work gloves and go down to tell the wood furnace a thing or two. To be sure, I had let the wood burn out and had to restoke it.

After recovering from that distraction, I began to recall some others that at given times and under the right circumstances can never fail to distract me from what I am doing.

Take the moth that flutters in front of my eyes on a cold November day in hunting season. In the first place, what is a moth doing out in such frigid air? My eyes are transfixed on his circling flight, and a buck might be standing within gun shot, for all I know. The same sort of distraction occurs in deer season when a squirrel makes noises in the leaves like a deer walking.

In the fishing season, it is difficult to keep one's mind on fishing when surrounded by black flies, or black gnats, or no-see-ums. This is a painful sort of distraction no matter how well one thinks one has prepared for it.

A more subtle kind of distraction is music in a restaurant. It is a rare restaurant that doesn't have music wafting gently o'er the mashed potatoes. There are times when my wife and I dine out without speaking to each other, for the simple reason that the music pounds our hearing aids with background noises that make conversation impossible.

A similar situation happens too often on the TV. Somebody is trying to say something, but the producer has smothered him with music. This beats on the hearing aid like surf hitting the cliffs at Bar Harbor. What the man was saying is lost in the roar of the surf.

This brings us back to the desk again. I had just finished polishing a sentence and was about to go to the next when from the road down below came "beep, beep, beep" repeated at intervals. The town grader is smoothing our dirt road, and every time he backs up there is the automatic "beep."

And now comes another sound from another direction, this time down the cellar, just below my feet. It is the pressure tank filling with water from the deep well—at first a gurgle, then growing to the noise of Niagara. I have never become used to it in fifteen years.

Country living is quiet around here, in between distractions.

Rx for Doc

A DOCTOR FRIEND of mine down in Maine retired a short time ago. That is, he took down his shingle, disposed of all office instruments and gadgets (some of them almost as old as he was), and went home to stew over not having anything to do.

He does do some consulting, and that's why he asked me not to use his name. So I'll just call him Doc.

He had been stewing around for a few weeks, crotchety as all get out, when his wife phoned me one evening.

"John, you better come over and talk this old so-and-so out of his doldrums," she said.

"What about his paintings? He went to an art class to learn about something to do when he would have a lot of time on his hands. Give him his paint brushes," I suggested.

She practically shouted: "In the mood he is in he couldn't paint the side of a barn door."

"OK," I said, "I'll drive over to Maine tomorrow afternoon."

Doc met me at the beginning of his driveway, just as I turned into it at the end of my trip. "Mary can't get used to having me around the house," he shouted. "I'm OK. She needn't have bothered you."

I made myself at home and just chatted about this and that for a while. But I had determined, on my drive over, to try to accomplish two things while I was staying at Doc's.

First, I wanted to get him talking about his practice, to look back on what feelings of challenge and accomplishment he had had at the New York hospital.

Second, I wanted to get him to laugh, laugh about himself and his experiences with some of the oddballs he had treated. Especially, I wanted to get him into a laughing relaxation. We used to have some good ones together.

I might confess here that I had just read Norman Cousin's

book, which had placed so much emphasis on how a planned program of the world's funniest movies had steered him out of depression and an almost fatal illness. "Laughter," the author had said, "is the world's best medicine."

After dinner Doc and I sat down in front of his fire, lit our pipes, and looked at each other.

"What the deuce did you bother to come way over here for? Just because Mary started yelping?" he muttered.

"I came because I think you are being a darned fool," I said. "You look as though you had swallowed a skunk."

Doc pulled all of his seventy-five years up straight as a rod and said, "You're nuts!"

"I was thinking about a time when you didn't look so sour," I said. "In fact you were a gay young blade and out on the town."

I reminded him of the time forty-odd years ago when he was taking some special courses at a New York hospital and I happened to be in town to sell some of our Stephen Daye Press books to that city's bookstores. I called him up, and we made a date for him to take the night off.

We were young and full of energy, and we hopped from one tearoom to another—the kind that served tea over long bars.

While sitting on our stools, I mentioned that my wife and I—both of us working in the publishing business—needed a live-in housekeeper and baby-sitter. This was something we were working on.

"I know just the woman," Doc said. "Come on, we'll go up and see her. She works as a cleaning woman at the hospital and asked me if I could find her a job up in the north country somewhere. She and her kid want fresh air."

We grabbed a taxi and went up to East 124th Street. It was about eleven o'clock, but the street was noisy with people. Entering the tenement house—dark, dingy, and with holes in the walls so that you could see right into the apartments — we found Grace Nubbins's door.

We knocked. A fairly good looking woman in a tattered nightgown came to the door. Doc told her why we were there and said that I needed a housekeeper.

To make a long story short, she arrived at my rural home in about two weeks. She immediately was homesick. Marion said, after a few days, "I wish she'd do something besides wash the sink all day."

Finally, after Grace had seen nothing but our trees, meadow, the brook, and blue sky for a week, she came to us one evening and said, "I got to go back to New York. I can't stand the quiet."

Well, Doc and I went on like that all evening, doing some remembering and some laughing.

He looked much better before he went to bed that night.

A Landlocked Sailor

In 1942 when Ned Jewell, former publisher of the *Manchester* (N.H.) *Union,* was in the office in charge of the First Naval District Intelligence Office in Boston, I met him at a newspaper meeting. Because of previous experience I had as a textbook salesman in all the towns and cities of northern New England, he asked me if I would consider applying for a commission in the Naval Reserve to do some intelligence work in those three states.

It didn't sound very inspiring, but because it came from such an "official" position in time of war, I discussed it with my wife and decided there was a form of duty involved, if I could get by the physical exam with my flat feet and one-half inch under minimum height of naval officialdom.

Commander Jewell assured me that part of my duty, after the nonsea operation in New England, would be a trip by water to England, where my newspaper experience would be involved. Being a Vermonter born on the Maine coast, I rather liked the thought of being a sailor. Perhaps it was my grandfather's years as captain of his sailing ship carrying granite from Stonington to Boston, for some of those old municipal buildings, that rattled around in my mind. Let's keep up the family traditions.

I mention this because during my war service I was on only one ship, and that was an overnight tugboat from Quonset, R.I., to New York. I did get a touch of salt water also crossing back and forth each day on the Brooklyn Ferry, during a few months I worked in New York.

Outside of that, my navy career was that of a landlocked salmon. After I had gone through boot camp and intelligence training units, I was sitting in my Vermont home on a weekend furlough from New York when a letter arrived that put me in a rather unique position. Over Ned Jewell's signature was the information that I "should immediately prepare my home for service as the Zone Four office of the First Naval District." It spoke of a tight safe, private phone, adequate door security, none of which I had. Seven other phones went on the line every time I talked with Boston from my rural home. I pretended for those months to being a recruiting officer and put my messages in those terms with the receiving officer. I actually enlisted a few men in the process.

In a few days I had received a series of assignments. Among them was to spend whatever time was necessary in the machine shops of Springfield, Vt. to make copies of all 1935–40 orders for tools sent to the Axis countries. I don't recall just what they were looking for, but it had to do with the capacity of those countries to build tanks, airplanes, and ships. By knowing what tools had been shipped by the three large shops to the enemy, before the war, it was presumably possible to estimate the size and nature of war equipment those nations could build.

All I know was that here was this lieutenant junior grade leaving his Zone Four office on Sunset Lake Road to bury himself in the old files of Jones & Lamson Machine Co., the Bryant Chucking Grinder Corp., and Fellows Gear Shaper Co. Their importance to the war effort is shown in the fact the town was listed 7th on the nation's list of possible bombing targets if Hitler ever nabbed England and went on to the U.S.A.

In my battered U.S. Navy Chevrolet, I would chug the forty miles north, in my beautiful blue serge uniform and white cap.

(Just how beautiful the nearly forty-year-old blue serge is was demonstrated by my youngest son wearing that old jacket as "dress up" as recently as five years ago.) When I arrived at Jones & Lamson I would say a bright good morning to the men in the front office and wend my way down to the basement. There, stack on stack of orders were examined, and copies were made and shipped by me to the First Naval District office.

I have no idea what was accomplished by this activity. I do know that it was hardly a seafaring job. I know also that those three shops, during the war itself, were five times the size they were before the war, and that they were basic in providing the lathes, gear-cutting machines, and grinders without which the makers of war equipment in the free world could not function. My basement days on prewar shipments may well have done some good, even though they didn't throw much salt spray in my face.

So, day after day for about six weeks I pushed my battle-ship to Springfield and back, while singing at the top of my voice, "I'm only a landlocked sailor, sailing the Vermont seas."

Three Men in a Tub

BUYING A NEW BATHTUB shouldn't be anything more difficult than replacing an old one. That's what we told ourselves last fall.

"No problem," we said.

So, we asked the young salesman, "What's new in bathtubs?"

Mind you, we were replacing a forty-year-old tub because it had to be replaced. There was no whim involved. We were perfectly happy with the old tub. It simply was no longer the tub it once had been. It had developed stains from hard water in copper pipes and had wilted under the attempted cure.

The "attempted cure?"

A friendly plumber had tried to help remove the stains by using a vicious acid. The acid took the copper stains out and corrugated the porcelain in the bottom of the tub. We are shower people, but, being older, we soak when our muscles ache. After the treatment for stains, the tub required a heavy towel to retain our skin while soaking.

So we were shopping for a new tub. "The thing today is fiberglass," the salesman said. He showed us a color picture of a shower-tub unit that looked "real neat." It came in four parts, looked light in weight, and was easily installed.

We noted particularly that the "components fit and seal perfectly," that there was "fast, easy and inexpensive installation," and that the exclusive molded-in structural ribs have the "strength and rigidity of a boat hull."

Certainly easy sailing, from here on in, so we placed an order for installation, come the warm days of spring. All winter long we turned up our noses at the old bathtub that had served us and a growing family so well for forty years. No compassion for it, whatsoever.

When April arrived we scheduled the day for the big changeover in the little, old bathroom.

First, it was necessary to remove the old museum piece. It wasn't easy. But we do now have the pleasant knowledge that a half-mile up the road, in a lovely hillside pasture, sits an ancient white tub beside the pasture gate where the cattle may line up and drink to their hearts' content. We can think of no happier retirement for that heavy steel and porcelain fixture. We hope that it is conducive to contented cows, heifers, and the new set of twin calves.

So we were then ready for the "easy installation" of the fiberglass replacement.

As noted in the brochure, it came in "four lightweight

components, easy to handle, and sealing perfectly for fast, water-tight assembly."

The brochure said nothing about no outlet for overflow. It did not mention that the drain was in the side and not the end, requiring a new pipe. It ignored the necessary synchronization of the efforts of three men — two plumbers and a carpenter — to get those "tight seals" of the four component parts.

The sagging floor of this house, built in 1842 and renovated in 1939, had to be absolutely level for this prima-donna bathtub-shower, so the carpenter dug in, landing somewhere between 1842 and 1939. The original house in the meadow had burned, and the neighbors had a bee to build one. As we looked at the skeleton revealed, we figured that the bee was held during the busy planting time of 1842 or harvest time. Those neighbors ran between planting or harvesting turnips and forgot where they left off, forgot to join skinny boards together or tacked a shingle over the gap. And there was not a single supporting timber.

"Wonder you didn't fall through long before this," said the carpenter as he went about the task of making a level floor. This condition may have accounted for those zing-and-crack sounds we have heard over the years on zero-degree nights. The bathroom was straining to get away.

Anyhow, the plumbers came back to a beautifully level floor.

At one point there were literally three men in a tub — pushing, lifting, pounding, and squeezing. It was right there we were ready to go out and reconstruct the little old house beside the lilac tree, torn down in 1939. Less convenient, but we would still be solvent.

But the "flexible fiberglass shower-tub" is now nearly installed. It is filled with blood, sweat, and tears, which presumably will be washed away when the outside water is turned on.

One thing it has done. It has shown clearly how we shall spend our remaining years — six months in the tub each year and six months in the poorhouse.

There is one consolation. My wife says that as the last connection is made she will feel like Cleopatra when she enters that towering white canopy because she will know it is not really white but gold, solid gold, as Cleopatra's was.

The Circus Boat Sails Again

THIS EPISODE HINGES on a note I received the other day from Robert L. Crowell of Newfane. He is a member of the family whose name has long been at the core of New York City book publishing. We knew each other years ago as young men in the book business.

"On pages 327–328 of *Guth: Letters of E. B. White,*" he wrote, "are references to that book you wrote about the circus that was shipwrecked off the Maine coast. Lawrence Langner and White were talking about making a musical play of it. If you feel like doing it, I think that a column on that episode might be interesting."

This was news to me, not having read the White Letters published a year or so ago. The book, *The Circus Boat,* was published in 1939 jointly by the Stephen Daye Press and the Junior Literary Guild. Thus, nearly forty years of lapsed time suddenly became alive with Bob Crowell's informative note.

Naturally, I went to the Book Cellar and got a copy of *Letters* by E. B. White to join all my other E. B. White books. He is one of the masters of the written word, known best years ago as the writer of the comments in the *New Yorker* magazine, which opened each issue with the special flavor of his style. Among books for children is his classic, *Stuart Little.*

"On page 327 of the *Letters,*" Bob Crowell had said, "is a letter from White to Langner, dated Dec. 29, 1950." It was to this I turned first.

On that date White wrote: "Thanks for your letter about a musical play. I do not have any material of my own that would be suitable. . . . Of course there are dozens of stories kicking around that have a Maine-coast background."

He then referred to the shipwreck of a small circus and said, "A children's book based on that incident was published some years back, I believe. If you want to look at it I can dig up the title."

Later, on Jan. 5, 1951, White wrote Langner, "The book you asked for was *The Circus Boat.* . . . It is now out of print. The library may have it in the juvenile department. . . . I am loaded with work now. On the other hand, I hate to stand up an elephant."

This takes care of the 1950–51 exchange of letters on a musical play, of which I was unaware until the other day. Nothing came of it, which does not surprise me. I find it difficult to see how *The Circus Boat* could have been turned into a musical play.

If you are curious, this is how *The Circus Boat* came about in the first place.

As a child visiting in Stonington, Maine, I had heard my roly-poly favorite Aunt Selma mention the wreck of a ship carrying a menagerie of circus animals that had been performing in towns along the coast.

I didn't know where it was wrecked, but when deciding to do a story about it in 1939 I chose Stonington as the town to which the circus unexpectedly swam. I let my imagination play as to the reception they received from the little fishing town and about the reward the town got in their later performance.

I think it was the Junior Literary Guild, to whom I had

submitted the manuscript, that located Charles E. Pont to do the illustrations.

After the book was published, a review in the *New York Times* noted that a ship called the *Royal Tar* carrying a menagerie had sunk off the Maine coast in October 1836. "This is a fact," the review said, "but the story is told with a simplicity and vividness which Noah himself would have appreciated. There is, however, a lightness of touch which is scarcely biblical in the author's account of the Captain, the Cook and the Cabin Boy, who took their troubles with a becoming casualness . . . and when lightning struck they put on their life-belts, let the animals out and swam ashore in a parade the like of which has never been equalled."

In 1939, when Charles Pont came to Brattleboro in the winter to help finish the book, he had asked for a chance to paint a winter scene of the house on Sunset Lake Road that my wife and I had just bought — a broken-down old farmhouse.

I picked Charlie up a few hours later, his long black hair encrusted with snow, with the water-color that still hangs over our fireplace.

I sit on the opposite couch, tonight, and think, "Charlie, wherever you are, just imagine that in 1951 our book got at least slight consideration as a possible musical play. You and I might have made it as dancing chorus boys in the back row."

I am content to glance left to the bookcase where our battered copy of *The Circus Boat* rests among our Stephen Daye Press collection. It made its way with the children for whom it was intended. That was its purpose and our only hope at the time — we had so much fun doing it.

I am especially content, after all these years, to know that a copy we recently obtained and sent to our English grandson has, at current writing, been requested for reading at bedtime on seven consecutive nights.

Chain-Saw Duet

LONG AGO, I TRIED to woo my wife into sharing my interest in golf. We had hunted together, so why not golf together? One day she dropped her small bag of clubs on the fairway and said emphatically, "I'd rather be home pruning." So that was that.

She returned to her recreation with the clippers and pruning shears. I continued the unproductive frustration of chasing the little white ball.

Actually, there was plenty of work for me to do around the place, too. Some of it I did — and still do — but I never was a pruner.

This was in spite of the fact that on one Christmas the family had presented me with a chain saw. I delighted to see the boys use it. Later I was happy when a neighbor's son found pleasure in odd jobs for me with my chain saw. I am still enthusiastic about what the sons do with it on occasional visits to the homestead.

Of course, the full-size chain saw was too heavy for my wife. What I did not know was that she bemoaned this fact. It seems that just as some women have yearned for years for a mink coat, my wife has silently longed for a chain saw.

In this recent fall came the answer to her longtime yearning. She had gone shopping for food and returned with two pounds of lentils (do you like lentil soup?) and with a chain saw.

"Electric," she crowed as she held the little monster before my eyes. "No problem starting it like our big one. It is light as a feather (but not quite) and it was on sale."

I had always dreamed that we would live out our lives with our own limbs intact. Now, I had doubts. In her seventieth year, my wife buys herself a chain saw.

She studied the book of directions with all the safety rules, however. In my estimation, a rule I suggested was among the safest: "Never use that thing alone—when there is nobody around to call for Rescue."

She agreed, and this is where I came into the picture. We started on branches that had been stored for cutting into firewood. On a crude sawhorse I constructed, the new saw went to work with a gleeful woman slicing off two-foot lengths of wood as easily as she slices dough. She soon developed the right "touch," just like a veteran.

"Now to those messy hawthorne trees," she announced a few days later. Have you ever worked around the spikes on the branches of a hawthorne tree? We soon learned how to do it, but not until having been speared a few times.

The first tree looked real nice, I must admit, after she had achieved the symmetry by careful selection of the branches. The next tree looked hopelessly entangled and I hoped our long cord would not reach it from the outlet under the barn. It did reach, however, and we moved into it, I alongside the happiest woman alive. She at last had the right pruning tool to tackle what had long evaded her.

Now, there is a hitch to this I hadn't counted on. What comes off a tree has to be picked up and carted to a brush pile somewhere. It was soon obvious that I had been elected to that part of the team, along with the little tractor and cart.

Perhaps I am more aware at this late date that there is more to pruning than just thinning out or cutting away. It is an art form, a shaping, or reshaping, of growing greenery that has gone berserk. It is bringing order out of chaos.

I am certainly aware of how much of it I have avoided over the years, while my wife had spent hours and hours each year with hand clippers accomplishing results I had merely taken for granted.

Take the lilac tree in the patio, which is between our breakfast table and the nasturtiums. Old photos testify that once the tree was large-based with a few branches, all of which broke down with child-climbing or snowstorms. Now the shoots have been shaped into a tree again and pruned so that we can also see the nasturtiums against the stone wall. All with clippers.

But there always have been trees around the house that needed pruning but were too big for hand clippers of any size. There even are some around the meadow where they can be reached by an electric chain saw from an outlet in the filter house of the old swimming pool. Winter is a good time to get at them when the leaves are off.

I'm no clairvoyant, but I see a new future for myself. I am part of a new team, led by a female pruner with an electric chain saw.

Footnote to the Theater

IN THE 1930s my wife and I were publishing books about New England subjects, under the name of Stephen Daye Press, and we were a small outfit. Our books were regional, yet we were able to distribute them nationally. It is amazing how many states contain nostalgic former New Englanders or former visitors to this region. They provided the base for a publishing enterprise that could print editions in sufficient numbers to make it worthwhile.

The small office, on Brattleboro's Main Street, overlooked the Connecticut River. It vibrated with ideas, some good and some easily discarded.

At that same time, there was another vibrancy in southern Vermont that, unlike regional publishing, has grown and spread into the number of separate enterprises that now exist in all the New England states. This was the summer theater.

One of the very early ones, in which metropolitan actors

tentatively sought audiences along the New England country-side, was the Brattleboro Summer Theater in the old coach house of the Estey Estate. The name Estey had for many years been famous throughout the world as a manufacturer of church pipe organs and family reed organs. The original old estate had been vacant for some time.

In the late 1930s one of the young actors in this summer group was Mel Ferrer, who was later to become well known as a movie actor and director.

Now, to go back a bit, I say we had a few good ideas in our Stephen Daye Press office about selection and promotion of New England books. One of them was the conversion of a Ford station wagon, vintage *circa* 1928, whose wood siding we took out and replaced with panels that could be lifted to reveal book shelves on both sides of the car. It became a traveling book store, with a driver-salesman who spent the summer taking it into the resort areas of Vermont, New Hampshire, and Maine. There was tourist trade, especially along old Route 1.

For several summers the old station wagon was sent out, stacked with books on such subjects as lighthouses, famous old New England houses, regional cook books, and the rather large variety of New England subjects we were publishing. Wherever it stopped to open up shop for business, it became a book store by lifting the side panels to form a pleasant sun-or-rain roof beneath which the customer could browse.

Now, back to the summer theater in Brattleboro, which was just over the fence from our house. Among the friends we had made in the theater group was young Mel Ferrer. It may have been one or two seasons he had small parts in the weekly productions.

I think it was about the third year he had been in the group, about 1938, when one day he walked into our publishing office and said: "I want to do something different this summer. I have

105

written a children's book you may be interested in. But primarily I wonder if you have a job for me in publishing."

My wife and I, our assistant Ruth Hard, and our salesman Sam Lincoln all looked at each other—with the same answer in our heads. I guess I was the one who spoke the words, something like this: "Mel, there are certain things about book pubishing one needs to know before finding the right niche. It happens we have successfully operated a book wagon throughout New England. We need somebody to take it out this summer. Would you like that job?"

Mel Ferrer blinked, but he took the job. He was a good salesman and said that it was one of the most interesting summers he had had.

It was some years later when we received a telephone call from Mel, at our home. He was opening in Boston as co-star of *Ondine* with a young actress named Audrey Hepburn. Would we like tickets?

We certainly would. What a charming and shy young actress was Audrey Hepburn. What a pleasure it was to see our star book salesman again, the four of us over coffee.

Beware of January

WHEN WINTER COMES, January can't be far behind. I am usually prepared for the whiteness of winter, but I never seem to anticipate that winter will include January, with its relentless encasement in icy cold air.

In its whiteness, winter offers the human spirit a vast variety of pleasures and excitement. I look forward to the ski trails on sunny days, and to the Northeaster blasting past the windows on a stormy day.

Fair weather or foul, winter is a season of contrasts. Its

snow can be enjoyed in the winter sports or it can be endured on the tractor plowing the hilly driveway down to the open road. It can have its ravishing moments of sunlight shining on snow-laden trees, or its discouraging embattlement with a car that has veered into a snow bank.

So, all in all, I find winter a variable season, keeping the spirits exercised by its challenges, its beauty, and its excitement. It is as good a season as spring, summer, or fall—and they add up to what is called the north country flavor.

But that excludes January—with its days and sometimes weeks that encase the human spirit in the bitterly cold stillness of an icicle. For me, it is no invitation to the subzero winds of the ski trails. Its clouded gray vistas hang monotonously around me as I rub my nose against its chill factor. I am aware of only one aspect of my surroundings—cold.

So I shall don my long johns this bleak January day. Where are the heavy ones? I need two pairs of mittens, that old scarf that makes me feel as though I had walked into a blanket hanging on a clothesline, a thick pair of socks in the lined boots.

How do you fit a cap's earflaps down over a pair of hearing aids, without their sounding like a pair of fire alarms?

Will the car start? It usually won't when the temperature is 17° below zero and has been lower during the night. I firmly pull the squealing car door open, push my downy bulk into the frosty seat, and push the accelerator down to the floor and release it, while I count twenty-five seconds before turning the key. This is a car-starting secret my wife passed on to me after some kind stranger from Europe had instructed her at a time when her car wouldn't start. Twenty-five seconds of cold anticipation as my boot rests on the floor. Turn the key. Wham! She starts, groaning a bit in the process.

By the time I get to the post office, my mittened hands are numb with cold. I open drawer D and fumble the mail into my illustration omitted for members.

nonfunctioning paws—open the door to get back to the car, and drop the bunch of letters in the gutter.

Ah, January! You who make it impossible to bend over in the clothes with which you have engulfed me. You who make probing fingers feel like icy-hot tentacles as they strive to rescue the fallen mail. You who strive your utmost to take the joy out of winter. How long, oh, how long is the month of January?

I should remember each year, before being taken by surprise. I should start thinking about Don Kent's upcoming January reports of "huge surges of Arctic air," and start anticipating the discomfort about the last week of November. And during December I should learn to do a better job of putting all long underwear, wool socks, padded pants, parkas, mittens, boots—all in one place.

I was still cold when I started home this January afternoon. I called my wife on the phone. "I'll be a bit late getting home," I said.

"Are you having trouble?" she asked.

"No," I replied. "I'm going to avoid trouble. I'm going to the sauna at the Action Barn and see what 190 degrees in the shade will do for me on this lovely January day."

Report on Wood

IN PAST WINTERS I have driven down the road and have observed the smoke curling from the chimneys of the wood-burners. Wood smoke gave an air of tranquility to each of these houses.

I have since learned that what one sees coming out of the chimney has little to do with tranquility. In each case there is somebody who has to stack wood, who has to feed the wood furnace, and who has to remove the ashes more often than seems possible.

109

We have been on wood for better than a month and are just beginning to think we can cope with it. We have eaten away at the piles of wood in the cellar and have had to replenish them twice from the supply under the barn.

In the meantime I have become (1) expert at getting out splinters, (2) permanently marked with soot on my left knuckles, and (3) possessor of a wry neck from peering through the door of the low furnace.

I want to point out that in the case of our furnace its care is handled by a partnership. My wife started off our experience with wood by volunteering to build the fire in the morning. Said she enjoyed it, and who was I to intervene?

Early in our experience we seemed to be getting more smoke than was necessary from the furnace door. It raised havoc with the living-room windows, worse than our accumulated cigarette smoke. So we asked the local stove manufacturer to stop by, which he did, accompanied by a helper.

Between the two of them they went over the furnace carefully, sort of taking its pulse. The verdict was that because of a down-draft in our part of the valley, we should keep the stack damper nearly open.

It helped, and we feel more familiar with all the draft controls.

We were not prepared, however, for what happened when Marion turned on the fan at the top of our front stairs. It is a powerful fan, used to draw out the hot summer air and pull the cool night air into the house. It is also used to clear the rooms of cigarette smoke and cooking odors.

I was sitting in a corner of the living room, reading. Suddenly I heard Marion calling, "John, John, where are you?"

I looked up from my book and stared into smoke so thick it was like fog blotting out Wadsworth Cove. I hadn't smelled the smoke because I can't smell.

"Where are you?" I shouted.

"I'm turning off the fan," she answered.

By that time we had to open all the doors and some windows — on a coolish day.

The fan had drawn smoke from the furnace and up the cellar stairs. Evidentally it pulled from the slightly open furnace door drafts. At any rate, the fan is not to be used as long as there is a wood fire.

There are those who love the smell of wood smoke. I don't know how it smells. Marion, on the other hand, has decided that the smoke from our furnace smells like finnan haddie. How it gets a smoked fish smell, being the result of burning dry Vermont wood, is beyond my ken. Perhaps we may be burning the same kind of wood (oak?) as the fishermen use to smoke finnan haddie.

At this particular moment I am sure the furnace needs a couple more sticks. I shall wend my way down the cellar for the umpteenth time. Between Marion and me we expect to wear holes in the cellar steps. Thus far I have only caught my heel twice because my bifocals got in the way between me and where I was going.

Did I say those plumes of wood smoke, rising from the chimneys, spelled tranquility? Forget it.

Skunks, Squirrels, Birds

THIS MORNING, at a downtown coffee shop, Pickles Bedard said that he saw two skunks around his place. According to tradition, this means spring is just around the corner. Those of us sitting around the table sipping our coffee felt relaxed — spring is just around the corner.

So, when I got home I looked around every corner, and I

couldn't see any signs of spring, I even remembered that we are on a waxing moon, which may be in Pickles's favor. But still no real signs.

Rather, I saw where the hungry deer, frustrated by the snow of 1978 and by the prolonged cold weather, had been as close to the house as twenty feet in order to eat the euonymus vine climbing the pole carrying our electric and telephone lines. I saw where they had taken advantage of the cold and hard snow to travel and to nuzzle under the apple trees fifty feet away, in hope of finding an apple or two. I hesitated to look in the barn to see if any of them had holed up there.

But Pickles says he saw skunks, and I am going along with him on the hopeful side.

Outside of the coffee shop I met René Columbus, a long-time printer friend.

"Has anybody seen any skunks down your way?" I asked.

René didn't hesitate a moment: "If they did, they probably saw me. In the mood I am in they might have been correct. I just learned that the motel on the Maine coast where I spend a couple of weeks every summer had a boat driven right through it by the storm last week."

So much for whether spring is just around the corner.

I know just what is around the corner of my kitchen. We have a Rube Goldberg system of feeding the birds. On a line through pulleys are all kinds of feeders, the predominant one being a deep cyclinder with holes and perches. One big gray squirrel found he could make it from the lilac bush. The first time he missed and fell to the ground and lay there like a prize fighter waiting for the count of eight. He recovered just before I counted nine, and he wobbled to his corner beside the lilac bush. Then he climbed it and jumped again, and made it. He was gobbling sunflower seeds by the pound. So, I had to begin calculating a solution.

I figured that if I pulled the whole rig six inches toward the house, with the rope securely hitched there, he could not reach it. He jumped and missed by five inches. I discovered birds don't mind eating on a slanted feeder, even up to thirty degrees.

Thus, the innocent little chickadees are back on the feeder, what part of it they can gain from the pugnacious pine cisterns who fill up greedily and who fight each other with the vigor of a young Spinks wading in on an aging Muhammad Ali. Above them sits a hairy woodpecker pecking away at suet like the financial promoter of any boxing show.

Speaking of red, we did somehow attract a cardinal with his mate, majestic against the white snow on the perch above the thistle seed feeder that hung among the assortment on our pulley line. Neither of them came back, and we suspect a neighbor of doubling her supply of thistle seeds or finding something she isn't telling us about. Would cardinals like chicken sandwiches?

As for spring, which at this point seems to be around several corners, the high water table in New England this year has produced its own kind of spring for us, a new bubbling spring of water where there has never been one before. It is right in the middle of that half of the area under the barn where we park the car and tractor. Naturally, the snow-blowing tractor has to have the dry dirt side. The car side has eight inches of solid ice where there is usually dry dirt. Who wants to let a car encase into eight inches of ice and dig it out in May? Therefore, the car occupies a place in the great out of doors.

In the meantime, we contemplate the eight inches of ice produced by the new spring pressing its water upward to be frozen. What was the name of the man from Texas who capped the spouting oil well in the North Sea? We are going to need a capper, when the thaw sets in.

Otherwise, I can report it has been a relatively quiet northern winter except for the excess of snow and ice. It has also given me the opportunity to see for the first time the vulnerability of heavy plastic waste cans against squirrels. The one we put the bird seed in, by the back door, was soon chewed through in a dozen places — first the cover and then holes in the top big enough to let an army into. Around the can was the evidence of green plastic shavings. I thought it was raccoons, until early one morning I saw both gray and red squirrels working on it like it was candy. The can there now is old-fashioned metal.

Outside the animals, though, it has been a quiet winter. I wonder what spring will bring. There are four seasons up here, and each has its idiosyncrasies. As seasons go, February feels better than January did. Is it from conquering the squirrels? Or is it skunks?

Down to the Sea

IT HAS BEEN a long winter on these seventy-five acres. The lack of snow has given a monotony to the brown meadow and to the bank that tumbles down to the road. In other years the snow had provided a variety to the outdoor scene. Each storm left a different imprint.

When an invitation came to visit on a Maine coast island and to go scalloping, it was like shedding the nearby hills and escaping to the more open spaces of salt water.

After a stopover in Portland, we proceeded to Rockland and to the ferry to Vinalhaven. It is indeed a ferry, carrying a dozen or so cars and trucks, but to me it is just a boat, and that is sufficient.

To stand on a boat, to feel it roll, to turn the face into the wind — these are sheer joy. They were heightened by the snowstorm that had developed the night before and persisted as we plowed through the sea toward Vinalhaven.

I was dressed in long johns, wool trousers, and my heaviest down jacket, yet I could feel the snow-filled wind reaching deep into my body. It didn't seem cold, however—it was the view in every direction that took me away from myself. Even the sight of the water through which the boat was pushing wiped out everything from my mind. Vermont and its strange winter had disappeared.

I had never seen the coastal islands in winter, and now I was seeing snow on the beaches, on the ledges and in the spruces. To one coming upon it for the first time, it was a wonder-world.

The passing islands, and there were many of them, seemed to push their spruce cover just above the water. Unlike the hills and mountains at home, I was looking out on the endless ocean. What was in the distance could only be guessed. What counted immediately was each island that slowly emerged from the distance until it was just abreast of us, usually guarded by colorful buoys marking the boat's course.

Finally, after about two hours of snow-swept seas, we approached Vinalhaven, impressive, largely white village with its own background of spruces.

Vinalhaven's harbor nestled with full protection within the side of this island. The boat slid comfortably into its slip, and the vehicles and passengers made their way to shore.

My group comprised host Bob Drake, former editor of the *Waterville Morning Sentinel* and executive director of the Maine Press Association; his longtime friend Jack Dowling, a columnist for the *Kennebec Journal*; and my son John, general manager of the Portland newspapers. As has so often been the case in my life, there was a tinge of printer's ink on the group of which I was a member. We hoped to swap that for scallop fishing if the weather calmed down.

At Bob's cottage a roaring stove soon brought out the simple

115

comfort of the place. With the reluctance of ledges to provide water, this necessary item was brought in plastic containers from a water supply down in the village. It was ample. A monument to waterless ledges was the facility that sat on a ledge high in back of the cottage and thrust toward the sky like a wind-blown lighthouse.

Dropping in at the cottage for lengthy conversations were Herbie Conway and Willie Olson. Herbie was captain of the ferry, and Willie was caretaker for several of the island's summer cottages. Somehow conversations turned to proposed increases in ferry fares, and both men were eloquent on the subject.

Our twenty-four hours on the island were coming to an end with the weather still against scallop fishing. Just before our return to the ferry, we had dinner at the home of Mr. and Mrs. William Minor, retired from Hartford, Conn., into the home they built. An added guest was Fritz Skoog, a long-time resident of the island. Somebody pulled from Fritz the account of his being nearly drowned when a tornado hit the small island where he was fixing lobster traps at low tide. Sudden twenty-foot waves picked him up, tossed him about, and deposited him on the shore, cut by giant barnacles. His eighty-odd years belie the experience.

I came back to Vermont with salt in the soul, good Maine conversation, and a bonus of a yarn about the treachery of the ocean.

After the Birds

THERE IS ONE spring chore we put off as long as we can, even though it stares us in the face every time we sit down to eat. It is a bit of leftover winter that lingers just outside the large glass doors through which we view the scene from our kitchen table. It appears after the snow melts.

Before the snow melts, and all during the winter, it has been a delight to turn our eyes from food to feathers. Over the rough slate patio we had strung our feeders in the fall. It was as neat as a pin then, and we looked forward to the pleasure that would result from sunflower seeds, suet, and various peanut-butter mixtures. One of the feeders is a hunk of Maine driftwood with holes bored in it by a grandchild. We wondered what curious bird it would bring.

All winter long we merely had to look. No effort in that, just sedentary pleasure. The feeders, the air, and the lilac tree, in the middle of the patio, were alive with birds — chickadees, nuthatches, woodpeckers, goldfinches, blue jays, purple finches, and once even a hawk. We eagerly lugged bags of sunflower seeds and bundles of suet from the store to keep them coming, the more the merrier. We waded out into all kinds of weather to keep their lunch boxes full. Then comes spring and a patio heaped with sunflower seed husks — and assorted other things. The spaces of soils and herbs between the slates are too wide to conceal the husks that have filled them and too narrow to sweep. If you have never tried to sweep soggy sunflower husks, you have escaped a vicious form of frustration.

We usually stand the unkempt and annoying sight just so long, and finally muster our determination to clean it up. Everything else around the house has been neated — bushels of wet leaves ferreted from the stone walls, the old wandering bittersweet vine cut back, the stone courtyard between the house and barn swept, even the lawn mowed.

But the patio and those tenacious sunflower husks offer a challenge that is not easily accepted. Believe it or not, it takes an old iron crowbar and three different kinds of brooms to obliterate this messy aftermath of what was an enjoyable winter

117

scene. It takes washing with a strong detergent and a vigorous hosing.

During this process, if a stray bird wings near, I bare my teeth at him — even though he may be the beautiful goldfinch in full colors, in contrast with his drab appearance last winter.

I say a strong detergent is used on the slate, but it takes a strong arm to work between the slates. Somehow I don't seem to have that kind of arm as much as I once did. Dragging the sharp end of an iron crowbar through a hundred feet of those spaces between slates is a job that takes about four hours and is, quite frankly, for the birds — for last winter's birds. It is the only way I know to dislodge wet sunflower seeds from moist soil. This discovery, after trial and error, may be some sort of scientific contribution to humankind. You may be sure that the next patio we have will contain firm cement between the flagstones.

I got the job done, and winter again, for another few months, is no longer evident. Instead of birds we see and enjoy a clean slate patio. We don't get the birds but we get neatness, which they say is a virtue.

Shall we or shall we not hang the feeders next winter? We doubtless will, as summer wipes out the memory of the frustration that thousands of sunflower-seed husks imposes on anyone who attempts to wrestle with them.

After all those hours of cleaning up, what the birds tossed away so nonchalantly and being ready for some kind of relaxation, I had found just one worm in the moist soil.

It was too few for fishing.

Autumn Ritual

IN THE AUTUMN it is hard to distinguish the joggers from brightly colored falling leaves. Joggers dress warmly in the fall,

118

and the enterprising manufacturers of sports clothes offer them many colors to choose from.

This is good. Jogging in nippy air demands a show of gaiety. Bright colors keep in tune with the alert and lifted spirits of the casual runner.

Here is a couple that outdoes the maple, birch, and oak trees lining the country road on which they jog. Her hat is a searing red ski toque with a blue tassel that bobs in rhythm to her moving legs. His hat is a brilliant orange, pressed against his red hair. Their sweatshirts are beige, like leaves of the ash tree. A series of colors flash from their shoes as they methodically pick their way along the leafy road.

Twenty-seven joggers passed my house already this morning. Some of them cast glances at the fall foliage as they jog. Others are lost in that kind of concentration which ties a runner to the staccato beat of feet against the road.

Thousands of joggers move along roads, sidewalks, bicycle paths, bridle paths, and fields these days. Why did it take nearly 2,000 years for so large a portion of human beings to discover the joys and disciplines of leisurely movement at a pace that lifts them from the walker into the realms of the runner?

I'll hazard a guess as to why. They are a recent product of the mechanics of free enterprise. They are the result of the kind of motivation that moves countless products into the hands of today's society. Had it not been for the discovery of science exposing the physical benefits of distance jogging — to the heart, the circulatory system, the mental mood — there would have been no doctors to advise jogging for one's health. There would have been no manufacturers of shoes, shorts, shirts, and sweatshirts to advertise and promote their health virtues. There would have been no magazines devoted to promoting the new faster-than-a-walk approach to health. There would have been no emphasis on this new life-style by the media.

Jogging is no less a product of our times than natural foods, vitamins, and the explosion of tennis from private clubs to a mass movement.

If it's good for us we have to be sold, or at least told. And jogging, done with the proper safeguards, has been one of the better products to come out of the current market.

Jogging, after all, is simply running. It is a form of individual movement that shifts from both feet on the ground at the same time — walking — to only one one foot on the ground at a time — running. Jogging is slow running — or running with ease.

Done for a mile or more, jogging is a way to lift one's spirits while exercising the body. Whereas jogging is primarily an individual effort, there are times when it takes on an added quality by becoming a group effort. It can be a unique form of socializing.

This is what I saw happen last weekend. On the sports page of the *Reformer* had been a small item saying there would be a four-mile run in Guilford, sponsored by the makers of Windermere Sprouted Wheat Bread. Each runner would receive a loaf of this special wheat bread made at the commercially enterprising home bakery of Mr. and Mrs. Bob Remy-Powers. It was the fourth annual run sponsored by the Remy-Powerses — a "come all and have fun" effort.

The fall day had a cold after-rain mist in the air. Leaves were falling along the country road, which the runners would traverse in a four-mile circle. And there were seventeen people, ready to run.

The oldest man was in his late sixties. There was one well-muscled man who used to be a good competitive runner in college, but told me that at age fifty-seven he was content to be a jogger. Most of the runners were in their twenties, and about a third of them were women. One couple started and finished the run hand-in-hand.

120

After the race, the joggers gathered in the Remy-Powerses' baking room — a spacious section of the rural dwelling this young couple designed and built. Bob Remy-Powers solemnly read the finishing times of the joggers, while each came forward to receive his loaf of Windermere bread. Most of them were strangers to each other, brought together to share their pleasure in a "good jog."

I received a loaf of bread — as the only spectator. I also had received a lift to my own spirits from sharing the warm simplicity that had brought these joggers together for an autumn salute to the one thing they had in common — a healthy addiction to jogging.

Deer in Meadow

WHO STARTLES MORE,
The deer or me,
Once I reach the meadow here?
The deer, nose-front, stand
Motionless in one small band.
I whistle a sound I knew,
Learned from a warden's crew —
A sound to come
And not to go.
It worked with some
Who perhaps were slow
To fear my whistled sound;
But then they white-tailed off
In one magnificent bound.

Deer are visible to householders on country roads primarily at twilight, when they feel safe to come from the forest to graze in the fertile fields — and, in season, to munch the apples.

What amazes my wife and me is that deer are so different from each other, in the same season. Some are dark brown, others are lighter, and then, of course, there are the spotted fawns. Even if we are not close to them — several hundred yards away — we get to know the habitual visitors to our meadow.

That dark, nearly black one. What is he or she, in hornless season, doing with the rest of the herd? Those fawns — which is buck and which is doe? We'll never know. But some fall morning we will meet one of them as a buck.

If we do, I am sure my recent shooting habits will not disturb him very much. I love to hunt, but I no longer shoot. Always in mind is the meadow. There the deer in my vicinity have found a foraging place. In the earliest spring, some seventeen of them. It dwindles down to four or five, sometimes one.

Speaking of one, there was the day in midsummer when I lay on my back in the ancient swimming pool, looking at the sky and enjoying relaxation. When I turned my head to the north, on the hill above the pool was a deer who, I imagine, was wondering what sort of glob of flesh was floating in the pool that usually was so quiet and placid.

We and the deer. We startle each other. For forty years we have been trying to know each other better. Whose fault is it that we don't? All I know is that deer, more than any other creature, intrigue me. They seem so sensible at times and at other times will bounce off into the woods for no apparent reason.

Do we hunt to kill, legally, for meat? We used to. I remember a well-planned expedition in which one group of us would start into the woods from a meadow opposite the pasture on the other side, in which another group would be awaiting the result of our drive. We beat on tin pans to make sure every deer in that stretch would know we were present. It worked.

The deer came from their hiding place and we had the chance, once in a while, to shoot at a buck. I have always maintained that in those earlier shooting days my rifle was bent—because I always shot around the buck they sent me. And, in retrospect, I don't mind who bent that rifle.

It all boils down to what you want deer around for. In the northernmost wilderness, it may not matter. A buck is a buck, if you have traveled that far. In our area, where there is more open land and the deer are more visible throughout the year, it does seem to matter to some of us. Even so, I don't post our land. My hunting habits are not justification for that extreme.

Last winter, a friend and his wife fed the deer near their rural home. One big doe would come within a few yards of a hand holding out a split apple. But not all the way.

The wild and the human are separate, but they can be friends.

Fireplaces

WHEN THE FIRST NIPPY DAYS of fall arrive, we know the time has come again for a fire in the fireplace. It is a preview of winter without the kind of relentless cold that winter brings.

A fireplace fire is built not just for a source of heat. It is also built because of what it does for the human spirit. Once the fire is burning briskly and the flames are leaping above the logs, I sit on a couch facing the fire and relax. By *relax,* I mean that there has always been something about a fireplace fire that starts me dreaming. As I look into the fire in front of me I see other fireplaces and their fires, over the years. I like to renew the warmth of those past experiences.

Right now, for instance, I can see again the big stone fireplace at my parents' summer camp in Castine. A seacoast fire of mostly driftwood is more colorful than the Vermont maple fire I am watching.

At Castine we often had a fire in the summer, to take the chill off a foggy day or just to dry out the camp. We boys found its warmth helpful after a swim in the cold ocean, standing nakedly with back to the flames.

As my wife and I sit here watching our own fire, she asked me what I was writing. I told her I was simply musing about fireplace fires. She said that in her girlhood she sometimes went with a group of boys and girls to Ginseng, a camp owned by Fred Harris, the founder of the Dartmouth Outing Club. The rule for the guests was that if wood were burned, the boys in the party would refill the woodbox. She said that the fireplace fire she remembered best at Ginseng was the occasion when her young man refused to help refill the woodbox at the end of the evening. She berated him on the journey home, and the evening was completed when he saw her to the door of her home. "See you in the funny papers," he said, and that was the last she saw of him. Interesting the good that a fireplace can accomplish!

There was the time when I was at the New England newspaper meeting in a hotel in New Hampshire. It was during this meeting that a hurricane swept through the northeast. It left us not only stranded for a couple of days but cold as all get out. We had been keeping warm by getting as near as possible to a large fireplace. It ran out of wood. The management said there was no more. Thus frustrated further, the gathering held an emergency council. Someone suggested that the summer furniture in the room seemed old and decrepit. It might provide a fire in the fireplace until the roads were cleared. Quietly, a group of stalwart citizens set up the furniture and broke it into the proper lengths. No fire ever seemed more friendly, and none ever sent out its heat with more zest, as the dry chair legs and caned seats burned with a crackle.

This is what has constituted my reveries as I sit here watching the apple wood I just added.

This is the year of the wood, and the winter in which I'll become the slave to the supplementary wood furnace down the cellar. From the amount of wood stacked around the house, one might think we are a log fort in the Revolutionary War. There are also aches and pains in every log stacked in those long piles.

As I said, the first fireplace fire is a prelude to winter, when the demands of a wood furnace will make this present little fireplace blaze seem the joy that it is.

To Make Life Hard

"ANYBODY SEEN MY GLASSES?" was my plaintive cry as I tried to get the cap off a prescription bottle. Either I am clumsier than the average person my age or I am approaching senility. Bottle caps, made safe for children (a worthy cause) completely bewilder me.

"Your glasses are on the dining room table," came the answer to my plea for help. I placed the bottle on a table and went for the glasses.

"Ah!" I murmured. Right in plain sight it said on the bottle cap: "While Pushing Down Turn."

So I stood the bottle on the table, my left hand around it, and my right hand "pushing down" and trying to turn the cap. It was no good. I left the bottle on the table, took a couple turns around the room to compose myself, and then made another try.

I was just about to go for a hammer and lo! the cap unscrewed as though it should have been easy in the first place. I was so relieved that I almost forgot why I was opening the bottle.

There is a variation on the push-and-turn bottle cap. This instructs me to "Hold Vial Cap Down — Turn." This one is easier, but until I learned how much pressure the left hand should put on the tab I was thwarted. I can report, however, that since I did learn I seem to be making progress in opening prescription bottles. I can even open an aspirin bottle in which you have to match two arrows—one on the top, the other on the bottle.

I wish I could say the same about milk cartons. On the whole they are easy, to be sure, but then I run into a streak of cartons whose spouts seem glued down. The only thing to do is pick away with the fingers. Gradually, a hole can be clawed big enough to get a finger into. By pulling down with the finger a spout appears. Or does it? When the milk is poured into a glass there is a stream on each side of the glass. A middle stream hits the target, but the whole business is a little messy.

As you may see, I am not adept at opening things. This is inconvenient, to say the least, for practically everything comes in packages or bottles these days.

Take packages of crackers or cereal. The top of the package is stuck down, and the directions say to slip fingers under the left and right side. This I do, as gently as possible. But the cover doesn't yield that easily. So, a little more pressure; and before I know it I have slit the top and destroyed the tongue that would fit in a slit and hold the cover together. This I have done for many years, always thinking I will exert just enough pressure to satisfy the box's manufacturer.

I also have a record of failure when it comes to opening a bag of cement or of cow manure. You know how they are. There is an impressive array of stitching across the top of the bag. I pull this little end, then that one, trying to find the open sesame that will let me get at the bag's contents. I end up by getting a knife and making a clear cut. To heck with the stitching.

If I seem to be preoccupied with container problems, I assure you that this is not the case. I can get just as frustrated with wrappings. I have yet to master the little self-sealing sandwich bag. No matter how I put the two sealers and press, I fail to come up with a sealed bag.

My most difficult problem is with a thin plastic on a roll, which supposedly tears off neatly on the jagged teeth of the box. Occasionally, part of the plastic adheres to the roll and doesn't get cut off. It may take a half-hour to figure out what is stuck and needs to be lifted from the roll.

If what they say about the little things in life being important is so, then there may be a certain importance in my struggle with containers. It may be a testing of my patience, or perhaps a way of helping my fingers to become more nimble.

Whatever it is, it is not something I can escape. I simply know that every medicine bottle, every container, every sealed bag is a challenge. Yet, I can't believe I am alone in this matter. Don't you have any trouble with these things?

Mountains and Me

DURING WORLD WAR II, when gasoline rationing kept Vermonters off the highways between towns — and kept tourists out of this state, period — I was a very much privileged traveler through Vermont, sometimes the only car on the road between, say, Windsor and White River or Rutland and Manchester.

On a special assignment through the state as a naval intelligence officer, my dirty brown naval car could pick up the gasoline necessary for the several thousand miles the assignment needed during several weeks. It was a rare experience.

Undistracted by the tension of driving, as it exists today, I could stop here and there and just look at the scenery, especially at the mountains. Just me and the Green Mountains.

Before ski areas had proliferated, I saw the mountains as pure scenery, as areas of wilderness, and as challenges for hikers, not skiers. I saw them as the backbone of a state noted for its stubborn courage in cultivating the foothills of these mountains, in using the streams that flowed from them for power, in providing occupations for those who floated their once-green timber down the streams to the mills for paper.

It was a unique experience for a person thirty-five years ago to be one of a handful of mobile humans who could look upon all of Vermont's mountains at a time when most people were denied—by wartime rationing—this blessed privilege.

In the meantime, some thirty years have elapsed since Vermonters reacted successfully against a proposal to construct a "skyline drive" along the tops of their Green Mountains. This was back when a greater percentage of the state's population was native Vermonters, before the Green Mountains were discovered by people seeking more elbow room than was available in the cities below, and before the thruways were built. Many have come and stayed because the mountains are here—those rugged ranges thrust against the sky with the valleys around them where villages grew.

Today the mountains are there for Vermonters to live with and for tourists to gape at. For some they are to climb, and for others they are to ski. But one senses that there is a growing belief that the mountains should be kept just about the way they are—untouched by further exploiting hands. Even skiers who cherish the thrill of standing on northern New England peaks, at the top of a chair-lift, have expressed the belief that enough is enough.

There is something about the mountains of Vermont, New Hampshire, and Maine—even something about their lower hills—that reaches deeply into all who cope with today's noisy and tumultuous routine of daily living. In the midst of a growing concern for a better environment, mountains become the exclamation point!

A coastal man in Maine, looking up from the clam flats, regards almost any promontory with a little bit of awe. Mount Battie, rising up from Camden harbor, commands respect from any saltwater native. People familiar with New Hampshire's sheer walls of stone in the Presidential Range feel the overwhelming closeness of this kind of mountain. And Vermonters, accustomed to the rolling foothills of the Green Mountains, hardly realize the height to which their mountain range really rises until they have stood at the top of Mansfield or Killington. There is a great diversity of mountains in this northeast corner of the country.

Each mountain has its own impact, depending on the temperament and background of experiences a person has brought to it. The beauty of none can be measured solely by its size. Each viewer is his own artist, his own poet—if that is the way he wants to look at it.

For everybody, a mountain is to some degree a symbol of aspiration, of inspiration, of contentment or excitement. It is something larger than life in its majestic simplicity.

"I will lift up mine eyes unto the hills . . . ."

"Peel Me a Grape"

I READ THE OTHER DAY that Mae West is going to do radio commercials. The announcement went on to say: "It is hard to believe, but true, Mae West, the eighty-seven-year-old sex symbol, has never done a commercial before."

If TV had been around fifty years ago it would have been able to catch Mae at her buxom peak. She would have filled the screen with her special physical attributes. Moreover, she could have sold anything from soap to lingerie.

Those old enough to have memories of Mae West's stage

and movie career ("Come up and see me sometime") are aware that the stage's body styles have moved toward the diminutive. There is nothing around that so amply fills a gown as did Mae West. All that and the glitter of rhinestones, too.

Reading further in the news story of Mae West's new career, I found that she will be appearing on behalf of Poland Spring Water. She says that she has been drinking it for twenty-five years, which might imply that it has been beneficial to her health. Something has.

It's a shame that she is to be confined to her voice only, on the radio. The TV screen would provide a fine opportunity to combine her sultry voice with the sparkling personality she must still possess. What if she is eighty-seven years old? So is Poland Spring Water!

Back in the heyday of the railroads, no dining car would be without its Poland Spring Water. I remember seeing it not only in the dining car but also as I walked through the train, seeing it in the chair cars. It had a long identification with railroads.

Now that it is being pushed as part of the new boom in mineral waters, I think I would like a bottle for old time's sake. It would take me back to the summer I worked in that massive, yellow Poland Spring House sixty years ago. This Maine resort was not only the home of the popular spring water but also a popular place to stay, a bit on the expensive side. My job was selling shoes in the small retail store off the lobby.

Among my customers were many as buxom as Mae, loaded with jewelry and with Mae's amazing physique, though without her blond-bombshell talents.

They made up a generation that held the health benefits of Poland Spring Water in high esteem. It is obviously Mae West's job to rise from that generation and convince the present generation of the virtues of Poland Spring Water. I'll bet she can do it, even if it is only her voice on radio. I'm sure she could do it on TV.

I'm writing this in Brattleboro, Vt., where, a couple of generations back, spring water was the foundation of one of America's outstanding water cures. In 1845, Dr. Robert Wesselhoeft established the Wesselhoeft Water Cure. This was an establishment in which the water was used as a physical treatment, through baths and running water from the springs.

One of the patients was Julia Ward Howe, in the spring of 1846. In a letter written to a friend at that time, she revels in the fine spirits with which she completed her series of baths. Had there been radio or TV at the time it is possible that this author of "The Battle Hymn of the Republic" might well have been urged to do a commercial.

As Mae West's commercials for Poland Spring Water hit the air, I shall think of that high hill in Poland, Maine, with the Poland Spring House on top and proprietor Hiram Ricker sitting in his surrey behind a pair of smart horses. In such a mood I wouldn't be surprised to hear again, from out of the past, Mae West's sultry voice saying, "Peel me a grape."

The Urge to Return

AT SOME POINT in the process of growing up, many people identify with a special part of their nearby surroundings. It creates a kind of fascination that draws them back to it, again and again. As they grow, year by year, this particular piece of the environment seems to become a part of them, to seep into their subconscious. In spite of all the distractions that may come later, and in spite of the distance they may be removed from it in adult life, there remains hidden within their inner selves a desire to return to the place that had so much special meaning for them in childhood.

It may be a hill that had loomed high above their rural home.

It may have been a patch of woods somehow preserved from development in a suburban area that escaped the proliferation of houses springing up in it. It may have been a craggy cliff reaching up from a lake or from an otherwise sandy seashore. Whatever it was, it was a "special place."

Those who became attached to such places in their childhood — and I am sure the experience was enjoyed by most people in one shape or another — never seem to lose the urge to revisit it. It lingers like the instinct of the homing pidgeon; it exists like the periodic signal that sends birds south in the winter and north in the summer. It is similar to the mechanism that turns a female salmon from deep ocean back upstream in a distant river for spawning.

Our own three children had the hill back of the house. It had to be climbed for exploration, and later for hunting. It grew into them and left its deep urge in later years — an urge to return whenever the opportunity arose. Sometimes there have been several years between these opportunities, but the hill has never failed to draw them up its side and (more lately) up its deeply wooded side that was once so open and green.

The daughter from England several years ago had hardly dropped her suitcase before she was off on a run for "the hill." Each of the two sons has headed for the hill, no matter how short his visit. At the moment, for the first time in twelve years, the two sons, now living many miles from their childhood home, are on the hill together — each with his own memories of why it fascinated him and now sharing discovery of the changes that time has brought to this special place.

It was a similar urge that for years, after I had moved to Vermont from Maine, found its satisfaction only when on occasion I was able to leave the closed-in feeling, which unfamiliar mountains at first produced, and to head for the ocean with its far horizons, seeking the beach and the clam flats on which I had spent hours of my childhood. It would be difficult to describe the sensory lift to the spirit when the first smell of salt air was reached as the car approached Portsmouth on its way to the too infrequent return to the special place that had so long ago become a part of me.

I am not speaking of simple nostalgia. I recognize that dwelling on the past and failing to be curious about the ever-changing present is a kind of ossification that must be avoided. This has nothing to do with "good old days" as compared with the world one lives in today and to which one should awaken each day with an open mind to the inevitability of change.

Rather, it is simply expressing one of the phenomena of life itself, the fact that at some time in one's growing up a certain tiny spot in a vast world seems to take on dimensions that separate it from all other experiences. It might be called the time and place when a human takes possession of a piece of the physical world around one, and it in turn takes possession of a corner of one's existence as a human being. It is one form of personal identification not only with the past but the present. It is one of the few forms of continuity in a world of change.

The two sons are back from the hill. "Saw two deer and a couple of hawks. Blueberries are spreading all over the top of the hill."

This is what they said. What is unsaid was that they had again experienced the enchantment of a piece of earth to which they once were so closely attached and to which always there will be the urge to return. It is where their roots are. More than that, it is where they have a special awareness of their roots. Return is a form of renewal.

Gambling with Books

BOOK PUBLISHING IS NOT an exact science. A publisher never knows whether he will make a couple of nickels on a book or lose his shirt.

So why does he publish?

I can only answer as a small publisher, some forty-nine years ago, when my wife and I and several associates were in the business because we thoroughly enjoyed it. It was our basic hope that we could make enough right guesses to offset all the wrong ones—we did need to make a living. For ten years, before World War II took all the men out of the enterprise, we made that living. The Stephen Daye Press, our firm, was a victim of the war, sold to New Yorkers at a time when we had no more manpower. It would have been too much to ask the three women remaining to weather the war.

Looking back to the question of why we published books, whose success was unpredictable, I shall take two titles about which we were equally enthusiastic. One was a dud, and the other was a success.

The dud could be blamed entirely on me. I had a personal interest in distance running. I was an admirer of the great Clarence DeMar who won the Boston Marathon seven times between 1911 and 1930.

It was my biased opinion that a book by Clarence DeMar about his long chain of remarkable victories, about his philosophy of life for one so devoted to physical fitness, would be a book that thousands would buy.

After all, didn't thousands watch him over the years as he ran the 26 miles and 385 yards from Hopkinton to Boston? I asked him to write the book, and worked with him on it. He was teaching printing, as he had for several years, in the Keene, N.H. teachers college, nearby.

It was a good book, called *Marathon,* and we had a fine representation in the Boston area stores. It was released on Marathon Day, and Clarence was still running.

All those thousands of spectators!

It soon was obvious that they (1) did not read books, (2) did not buy books, and (3) did not need a book to see Clarence DeMar plod his way past wherever they may have been standing.

I learned a few things from that book, but I am still a great admirer of Clarence DeMar.

Now to the book that was a success, even though none of us at Stephen Daye Press would have guessed it. One day our supersalesman, Sam Lincoln, who was the spitting image of Robert Benchley, brought in a manuscript in which there was not one word. It was made up entirely of illustrations and depicted the subtle (and not so subtle) changes in a woman as she went through pregnancy.

Unlike DeMar, its author was unknown. She was a young woman in Springfield, Mass., named Betty Bacon Blunt. She had given to her book, with no words, the title of *Bet It's a Boy.*

We decided to promote it with a mailing list of doctors, as a humorous but authentic account of pregnancy. In addition, we advertised it as the kind of book one would like to send, instead of a card, to friends who were in the hospital about to have a baby.

All of a sudden, we had a best-seller on our little hands. The book took off into a sale of more than 50,000 copies in the first year, and it did equally well for several years after that.

I am not sure, at this point some forty years later, but I think the book is still in print on some publishers' list.

Publishing? It probably is done these days by accountants with computers. There was a time when some of us who are neither accountants nor computers had fun at it.

The River

We looked at the package in the middle of the living-room floor. Its heavy brown paper was torn in places. Its shape resembled what might have been half an Egyptian mummy.

We knew roughly what it was, even though we had almost forgotten in that spring of 1934 that a book publisher in Austria had months before written that he was sending an Austrian falt-boat in payment for the right to translate and publish an outdoor cookbook off our Stephen Daye Press list. This, he said, would avoid the rigmarole of foreign exchange if paid in cash.

A falt-boat, about which we knew nothing forty-five years ago, seemed an intriguing form of payment. These little canvas boats shaped like an Eskimo kayak were hardly the rage then that they are now on fast-water rivers all over the country.

So we gazed at the package and then started opening it. It soon was apparent that there was considerable assembling to be undertaken. The wooden frame needed to be put together with our inept skill and inserted into the canvas for support, in order to transfer chaos into something that had a bow and a stern, that looked like a boat, and that had room enough in it for two people to sit with their bottoms separated from water only by the wooden slats and canvas. A canvas cover with two holes for the passengers formed a protective deck against water's pouring into the little craft.

It was as light as a feather, and each occupant had a double paddle whose ends were dipped alternately, from one side to t'other, to move the boat through the water—swiftly, as we later found out.

After the hours it took to put the thing together, having cracked only a few slats, it seemed at the time that a better policy of payment for foreign rights to our little publishing company's books would be cash on the barrel-head. But weeks later we reassessed our thinking on the matter — the falt-boat justified our original policy.

It was late in May when we tied it atop the *Blue Swan,* our bright blue Ford Phaeton. Its lightness didn't even dent the canvas top of the open car.

We headed north, up the Connecticut River. When we reached Hanover, N.H., some seventy miles upstream, we hired a garage man to join us on the next leg of the trip where we would dunk our unknown craft in the river. At that point, the garage man would leave us to our fate and take the car back down to Hanover. Hopefully, we would meet him there the next day, twenty-five miles downstream.

Away went the *Blue Swan* and into the river went our little canvas peapod. We settled our bodies into it, with a couple of thermos bottles and a little food. It was just after noon, and we were somewhere below Bradford, Vt. Our plan was to take our time, enjoy the lovely peacefulness, and keep our little craft upright and afloat.

Seated so low into the water, my wife and I immediately felt that we were part of the river. Such serenity! Not a sound except birds, accompanied by complete eyefuls of beautiful spring colors wherever we looked under that clear blue sky, in the winding part of the river.

By dusk we had worked our way down to Fairlee. We beached the craft and started through a cornfield toward a farmhouse. Suddenly a man hailed us and wanted to know who we were and what the heck we were doing in his field. We decided the better part of valor was to keep walking to him, and we were right. After hearing our story, we were given a glass of milk and some fresh doughnuts and directed to a house that took overnight guests.

The next morning, at daybreak so as to enjoy the fresh mist on the river, we headed for Hanover and the *Blue Swan.* Those two days were an adventure in being alone on the big river and in enjoying the form of payment the Austrian publisher had so wisely chosen. He knew from his own European rivers what we would experience.

Our book publishing days of forty-five years ago had few dull moments and many pleasant surprises. None of them could be savored so fully or for so long as does the remembering that this river of many moods once treated us to its very best one.

We forgive it its turbulent freshets and floods. We remember its embrace—so unexpected, so heartwarming, so long ago.

My One-Carrot Garden

WHEN WE FIRST CAME to this place forty-one years ago, we had vigor. That is, we had more vigor than we do forty-one years later.

At that time we possessed only the ten acres of open land around the house; the hilly forested part was acquired later. All that open land—to us, who had been living in apartments— simply cried out for gardens, big gardens.

We grew our own potatoes and apples, and we had vege- tables to can and fruit to turn into jellies and jams. This went on for several years.

Not being farmers but publishers and newspaper people, however, we increasingly had less and less garden time. We began to cut down the size of the gardens. Then, finally, came a time when we had merely our berries, an asparagus patch, and some rhubarb. We were too busy downtown to do otherwise.

My wife has stuck to her flower gardens, which are her love and joy. I hadn't put a spade into a garden until, last spring, I decided it might be a good thing to have a little garden to grub around in.

So, Oscar, down the road, brought his little tractor and

rototiller up and plowed my garden spot, just beyond the raspberry patch. It looked mighty small when he finished, but I had told him 10 feet by 10 feet, "just big enough to turn in."

Deer and woodchucks being what they are around here, I put up a wire fence. By doing so, I learned when "little" becomes "littler." It was like jumping into a rabbit hutch.

What should I plant? A few carrots, maybe. Lettuce, yes. And tomatoes, of course. It would be nice to have a few beets and brussel sprouts. Cucumbers and summer squash.

These were what I thought as I raked the little fieldstones around in the enclosure, my buttocks against one fence as my rake did its work near the other.

Josephine, another neighbor, gave me some leftover seeds from last year, and I bought enough more packages to fill out the rest of my master plan. Naturally, also, I put neat white sticks at the end of each row on which I could slip the seed packages, to know what I had planted and where.

The little buggers were hardly out of the soil before winds came and blew away my markers. I had forgotten what was in half of those neat little rows.

"I'll wait and see what comes up," I said to myself as I pulled away at the scrubby weeds. I waited. The rows gave up their plants to the sunlight, but what the sun was shining on I don't know yet.

"I'm sure this is a kind of lettuce that Josephine gave me," I muttered as I examined the strange leaves. "And this must be beets," as I paused over leaves that didn't look like any beet leaves I ever saw. I don't know what they are yet; and here it is the last of August.

It may be that these plants in my garden are affected by the fact that when I drove the tomato posts in I found I was on part of the ledge that comes down from the hill above. Do three inches of soil resting on a ledge make plants grow differently? Is it that their struggle to survive puts new twists in their vines? Or were Josephine's opened seed packages full of seeds different from the name on the package?

Of course, I know where the cucumbers are. They'll be ripe for picking in December. The squash will never make it. And the Gilfeather turnips must have their noses plumb against that ledge, because their rumps are four inches above the soil.

Anyhow, I have found one carrot bigger than a penknife. I wiped it off right there and ate it, as I whispered to myself, "Who said I don't remember how to grow vegetables?"

Remember How Winter Smelled?

YOU COULD SMELL WINTER in Maine when I was a boy, especially in its small towns. Now winter is a cover-up, a white one if there is snow, and those cold-weather odors of a half century ago have since been wafted away by the winds.

Smell winter? Certainly. Just walk into any stable in my town, and there were many of them, and the strong fragrance of ripening venison greeted you from the six-pointer suspended from the rafters.

Once you had walked into one of these stables in December or January, that particular winter smell didn't leave you for a while. And each year it was expected as part of the season. The deer brought in from the deep woods each fall could only be kept by exposure to the winter air, month after month. There were no freezers into which they could be neatly cut and packaged, to exist as they do now and bringing now no other odor to winter than the smell of the paper in which they are wrapped. No real gamey smell to give winter its bouquet of forest and dry leaves and a hunter's lingering reminder of his skill with a rifle.

What a contrast it was tonight between what I saw years ago in Herbert Norris' stable and my going down cellar to pull a rib roast of venison from an innocuous freezer. Each winter night when I entered the Norris stable to feed my pony I was greeted by a gush of pungent aroma from the buck that was providing the Norris' Sunday dinners.

Winter these days is pale and undistinguished from the snow in which it is wrapped.

In the elementary school that I attended, most of the pupils came from farms. That is, the family kept a cow or two, chickens and a few pigs. The schoolhouse was kept airtight to keep it warm from the big coal furnace in the basement.

You could smell winter in that schoolhouse. You know how cows smell in the winter, or did before all this super-hotel environment in which they now spend their winters. And the chicken houses, little ones that the kids had to clean out after school.

On a real snowy day, when all the mackinaws and wool scarfs were hung up on the hooks outside the classroom, you didn't have to know there was snow outside in order to decide it was a winter day. The smell of winter hung right there on those hooks.

There are certain smells of those oldtime winters I miss very much. I am an admirer of horse blankets, especially after a horse has worn it for a couple of winter months. I don't know how to describe the pleasure it gave me in my pony's stall except to say that if you have seen, as you must have, all those TV commercials in which rapture is shown over the fragrance of whatever is in the little bottle at the cosmetics counter—if you have seen those sensuous scenes you have seen me in my pony's stall on a winter's day.

There are other long-ago winter smells, however, that I can do without. I never could abide the camphor bag my mother hung around my neck to keep me from catching cold. Nor the mustard plasters when I really did have a cold. To be sure, I could wear them today because I have lost my sense of smell. But other people might not like it. Just as some pretty young lady may look at me with a nasty frown when from her nearby table she spies me lighting my after-lunch cigarette.

There was a fellow the other day who said in a magazine article that the sleigh rides of his youth were for the birds because he couldn't stand the smell of a buffalo robe.

Now I don't know where the buffaloes came from whose robes he rode under, probably from Australia, but my buffalo robe and all of Uncle Warren's I snuggled into were the essence of sweetness—of how any winter should smell.

Beloved Jeep

OUR HILLSIDE HAS NEVER seemed quite the same since we foolishly sold the jeep twenty years ago. It had become a part of the family and was regarded with affection. During the fifteen years that the jeep was serving us, it was at one time or another in the hands of all members of the family. In fact, if we still had the jeep I could turn over the snowplowing to Marion. She did more plowing than I did because she thoroughly enjoyed handling the little blunt-nosed car.

We had bought the jeep as an instrument to help us live through the four seasons. This it accomplished, plus other contributions beyond the call of duty.

When Johnny was approaching the driving age it was reasonable to let him drive the jeep around the meadows and up at the base of the pasture. Here he could maneuver to his heart's content.

It was not until quite a while after that I learned that when he had graduated to the plateau he and his friend Billy Cushman carried on a series of war games. They would head the jeep into a patch of juniper bushes or at a young pine tree, whooping as they roared over the enemy.

It was unnecessary to teach our children to drive, after they were made aware of the jeep's limitations. The vehicle itself was the teacher. When they were old enough to go on the road, they did so with assurance and with respect for what they were driving.

Our house needed an addition to the stone wall on the brook side. With Johnny driving the jeep, we were able to rob some of our more distant walls. It took a half-dozen loads, which he and I fitted onto the old stone wall. The fact that he could work alongside of the jeep took care of the motivation.

The whole family participated in haying. The equipment comprised the jeep pulling an old McCormick mowing machine. After the grass was cut and allowed to dry to hay, we all used large wooden rakes to pull the hay into windrows. Then the hay was loaded onto a platform-trailer pulled by the jeep. Hay also was piled high on the back of the jeep and finally on top of the

144

driver's compartment—with the jeep looking like a moving haystack. Only the driver could see where the stack of hay was going.

Because I had elected myself driver, I had to make up for it by hard work in the barn. I had to get into the haymow and stack the hay away. Needless to say, I didn't elect myself to this job.

When spring started the sap in the maple trees on this place, a large, old collecting barrel was put in the back of the jeep, and it was possible to drive to the hanging pails of sap. With a quarter-size evaporator in the back yard, enough sap could be drawn from the collecting barrel to boil into syrup.

As you may see, we had reason to develop a fondness for the jeep. It was practically our common denominator over a period of years, during the growing period of our children. It was not my jeep or her jeep, it was our jeep.

When Mary Ann, five years younger than Johnny, reached her turn to drive the jeep to high school, the battered old vehicle had lost its battle with Vermont salt—there was no longer a floor; the seat was tied firmly with bailing wire; the canvas cover was torn to shreds.

Yet Mary Ann would have been disappointed not to have the pleasure and independence of driving to school. In winter, wrapped up like a mummy, she would brave the cold and wind in an open-ended jeep. It probably was good for her alertness when she arrived at school. One of her teachers said, when Mary Ann came up the walk, she always thought that she must be a student from Alaska.

So, there it is, our jeep. It is sadly missed ("I'd plow if I had the jeep," says Marion), and it is remembered with utmost affection.

What's a Barn?

I READ AN ADVERTISEMENT the other day offering to find me a barn if I wanted to live in one. It said that the company was prepared not only to find the barns but to move them to whatever site you might choose and to convert the barn into a home according to your liking for modern conveniences and decor.

The ad excited me because I have always had a lingering desire to live in a barn. I like barns and have spent a lot of time in them. For those childhood days when I helped Uncle Warren milk in the moonlight, watching Silky flick her tail and the moon flick the waters of the cove at the same time, barns have seemed homey to me.

Apparently, others feel the same way or they like the kind of barn structure that fits into the soil. At least there is an enterprising company that has found some who think this way and hopes to find more.

I can understand this frame of mind, because a barn has always seemed a welcoming place to be in. The welcoming part has been the obvious contentment of the cows, horses, sheep, or whatever animals were living there. I have liked the way barns smelled—from the hay, from the animals themselves, and from all the other things that smell like a barn: from oiled harness leather to manure. The beauty of a barn is that these smells are not separate but merged, and together they have a special aroma.

I don't suppose that this is what the company selling barns for homes is referring to. I suspect it confines itself to the attractive, simple architecture of barns, plus barn boards.

As for our own barn and why I am not living up there, the answer is simply that there is not enough space left for me to fit into living quarters. The time has passed when I could have moved in with the horses, the heifer, the goats and pigs. The loft was full of hay, then, and I could have found myself a comfortable shelter in the hayloft and enjoyed the company of the animals. Things are different now.

A barn, by definition, is a shelter for animals, crops, and wagons. Ours fitted this definition, if you consider that we had the pigs and wagons under the barn. Now they are all gone, and the barn is simply a barn structurally. I suppose it could be moved to a site with a better view, or proximity to a lake or seashore—but I would hate to see it happen.

Over the past twenty years, our barn has taken on a usefulness and character all its own. It has become the storage space for the kind of things we probably should have got rid of years ago. The accumulation of worn-out goods is beyond belief and not necessarily something we brag about. But they are there—from childhood sleds to outgrown skis, from the office files of a recently retired newspaperman to the harness and horseshoes of an old mare long since retired, from a Franklin stove that a great aunt in Bangor found for us before we were married (and needs a new back) to rugs, old tents, and cabinets that never will be used again but which each year we think it would be a shame to throw out, from nuts and bolts to wooden rakes and lawnmowers. The old barn simply demands to be used for storage, even for memories—the sheepskin jacket of a ten-year-old hanging in the corner of the tool room, the fifty-five-year-old track shoes nailed to a wall.

A barn is by definition a shelter for animals. It may take on a new dimension as a shelter for people, but our barn shelters things that have been part of our lives and that we are not about to be tossing out.

Even with the animals gone, it's a barn by our own definition. Still smells like one, too.

Easter Parade

WHEN WE REMODELED this farmhouse, we made sure that there were plenty of windows. We wanted light in the house, but, more than that, we wanted to see our surroundings. There were windows from which to see the brook and the road. Others let us look at the woods from different angles. We could be inside and still have an affinity for outdoors. That's why we came here.

We did well with most of the house. We lost our touch with the kitchen, however. Expediency dictated our remodeling there. The sink had to be in a certain place in order to drain properly into all the connections to the septic tank. That meant there wasn't much choice as to where the cupboards and refrigerator would go. There was less choice about locating windows. Consequently, there was only a small high window facing the meadow, the most open area to see.

We corrected this in a second remodeling about twenty years ago. We were able to rearrange cupboards, sink, and shelves to make the space we wanted for a large window facing the meadow. In fact, we took the whole kitchen from darkness to light by adding two large glass doors, facing the old lilac tree in a new patio.

Now we could feel that we were practically outdoors in a useful kitchen. Through the glass doors we could watch the gray squirrels, the red squirrels, and occasionally a flying squirrel. We had the jays, chickadees, nuthatches, and various woodpeckers only a few feet from the lilac tree, birdfeeder, and suet basket. Through the picture window we looked out on the meadow, often lively with unexpected wildlife, a meadow changing color with the seasons, changing its moods with the daily weather.

It was from the kitchen that we counted seventeen deer last spring, in one herd. It was from here we watched fawns play around their watchful mother. Even the appearance of a wood-chuck, sitting up straight on his haunches to scout the area, was fascinating.

The kitchen window has framed many deer over the years. This morning, however, it framed a picture I have never seen before.

I had come down to the kitchen for my cup of coffee. Then I pulled up the insulated curtain on the big window. (All that glass doesn't help the energy problem; the curtain does.) As is my custom, I gazed out into the meadow, scanning the woods at the lower left and the bank on the right. I thought I could see something moving up on the bank, but I couldn't make out what it was. So I went back to drinking my coffee, standing sleepily by the window.

Alerted, I shouted to Marion to come and look. At first, I could hardly believe my eyes. Marching down from the bank were four wild turkeys, obviously a family. The gobbler was in the rear, the hen was in front of him, and two smaller turkeys led the march. I am guessing they were about a year old. Even the youngest seemed large. They were close to each other, in an absolutely straight line. They walked very slowly, looking directly ahead, turning their heads only enough for their eyes to keep track of what might be around.

As they walked past the window, not more than twenty feet away, the only motion seemed to be their primly lifted feet and their heads jerking forward and backward. Their whole appearance was dignity personified.

Past the window they marched, with another fifty feet to go to the bank facing the road. They were serene in their mottled gray colors, with the touches of red on the gobbler's head. They kept their formation intact. That is, they did until they reached the bank, spread their wings, and flew over the brook into the woods.

It was the day before Easter. We had had our Easter parade.

From Steam to Rockets

ONLY A FEW YEARS AGO Dick Mitchell had a boat on the Connecticut River, which he would ply on the generous expanse of water between the Vernon Dam and Putney, just for fun. Ever since his navy days, Dick had become a steam buff, and the boat he operated was equipped with a steam engine he had acquired from a launch that some years ago did its quiet gliding on Spofford Lake, over in New Hampshire.

From time to time I could watch his steam craft through the windows of the newspaper office on the Vermont side of the river. Little did he know what this sight meant to a State-of-Mainer transplanted to the inland river with its background of the Green Mountains; especially what his steam whistle would evoke as he occasionally would pull the cord as a sort of salute to the stores and offices along the Brattleboro "waterfront."

Dick Mitchell's craft was that steamer sailing out of Rockland, Maine, years ago, headed for Castine where as a boy I spent my summers in the little coastal town where I was born. My father took the family there each year during his three-month vacations. Teachers didn't have to worry about going to summer schools for recertification then.

His little steamer was also a piece of the story my mother occasionally told when she described the night the *Goldenrod* nearly foundered in a storm on a trip from Castine to Stonington, when the chairs and tables rolled from one side of the little ship to the other.

It was the nightly docking at Castine when the *Pemaquid* would attract half the citizens of the town down to the wharf to see who was coming and going and what was being landed to be hauled by Uncle Warren's long "jigger," which was a seaport vehicle comprising tough boards hung below the axles so that freight could be rolled directly from the steamer's deck to the cart, drawn by a pair of horses and serving the few industries in that resort town.

Dick's small steamer on the Connecticut was also the great *Majestic,* one of the "up and down," transatlantic, turbine-driven steamers on which my wife and I returned in its steerage quarters from our delayed honeymoon walking trip through England in 1932. It was the *Majestic*'s last voyage, and we were broke, having exhausted the little funds I had saved from my premarriage employment as a textbook salesman. Steerage was the cheapest passage home, and like the wonderful immigrants with whom we shared those quarters deep in the stern of the ship, we were stood in a chair under a bright light when the ship docked in New York harbor and examined by immigration officials to make sure we were not transporting lice into this "Land of Opportunity."

No, Dick did not know these things that went through my mind as a Vermont newspaper editor looked out his window at the tiny steamer passing by on that short stretch of the Connecticut River.

Steamboats, once in abundance in all sizes for coastal or transatlantic business, are a part of history. They had their day, as did the cargo-carrying sailboats. But that little steamer of Dick Mitchell's on the Connecticut River had all the history of "steam" in one toot from its authentic whistle. There had been no other sound just like it.

Of course, there are still some steamships in limited operation. And Dick—whose Hinsdale, N.H., home is filled with colorful pictures of the old-timers and houses, the little whistle I used to enjoy hearing—estimates that there are some 200 steam "hobby launches" operating today on lakes and rivers scattered around the nation.

Of such is the evolution of "energy" for transportation on land and sea and into outer space. As Dick put it the other day,

"The airplane killed the liner in the same way the railroad killed the stagecoach and the automobile killed the train."

To Market

ONE OF THE BENEFITS of retirement for the man of the house is to take over, on occasion, his wife's grocery shopping. During all the years he had his nose to the grindstone he had accepted the fact that somehow his wife came up with the groceries, week in and week out. In my own case, I went through a number of trial runs, accompanying my wife. From her master list of items, she would give me two or three to ferret out.

Mind you, we were in this huge building covering several acres. Row on row of groceries loomed like a virgin forest. Thousands of items, plus many versions of the same item, filled the shelves awaiting the unwary hunter.

Among the few on my first list was Colgate toothpaste. I found the section containing toothpaste and looked for Colgate. After my eyes had crossed and uncrossed several times, and just as I was about to grab any tube I could reach, I spotted what I was looking for. I felt as though I had won a cross-country race, tired but pleased.

So now I could go to the second item on my list, sour cream. I walked up and down in front of the refrigerated dairy products. Package after package looked almost like all the rest. Finally, I found sour cream nestled up next to yogurt and only inches from all-purpose cream.

The third item in my trial run was cream-of-shrimp soup.

Ah! Here was a delightful dilemma staring me in the face. How many kinds of soup there were on those shelves I'll never know. I do know it didn't do me any good walking up and down in front of the soups. It was necessary to lean over, to stand on tiptoe, and to remove at least a dozen cans for closer scrutiny.

At last I could start looking for my wife in this vast cement and steel tent. I felt like a golden retriever that had been sent to fetch a stick, whereupon he brought the stick to his master, with a good deal of tail-wagging.

Having found Marion, I presented the three items with a bright grin of accomplishment. Then I looked at my watch: it had taken twenty minutes.

After a few more training periods, including working closely with my wife as she explained the layout of the supermarket, I was at long last handed the total list and sent forth on a solo flight. I first made sure I had a pencil, indispensable for crossing off lucky finds. I drew off the highway on the way to the market to become thoroughly familiar with the list. Marion had helped by listing the items roughly according to the rows they would be in.

Once at the market, I grabbed a cart. Right off, I realized the cart must be handled gently to turn properly. On the whole the cart acted well, but I cut one corner too closely and scattered a pile of special cereals. This was on my way to the first item.

At the meat counter, which we had always avoided for reasons of economy, I was looking for a small beef tongue. There wasn't any in the case. How to find out, with no clerks around? I finally noticed a bell, and everything was taken care of efficiently and pleasantly. It does seem good to have a clerk to talk to in the midst of all this self-service.

It took me about an hour to get the list of twenty items. I got bogged down in vegetables. I never saw so much cellophane before! What was inside, besides the dead-looking lettuce?

As I passed down the canned-fish-and-meats aisle, I met an old friend, retired, and his wife. In soap I met another, also with his wife. I guess they were in some stage of their training schedule. There were other men, either in training or on their own. I was rather pleased to be a step ahead of some of them. I think I could be called a tenderfoot, without the badge.

Naturally, my arrival home was a triumph. I did feel I had done rather well. It wasn't like getting a newspaper off the presses and onto the street on time, but it was a somewhat similar feeling.

The Skier in Green

THIS MAY APPEAR to be an essay on skiing. It isn't, for many reasons. Among them is the fact that while many people enjoy skiing beyond their youthful years, both downhill and cross-country, many more don't. So don't stop here if you are not a skier.

This is an essay on incidents that stand out in one's life. In this case it happens to be a skiing incident, after retirement, that took place on a bright, cold winter's day at Vermont's Stratton Mountain. It stands out because of the beauty it involved and that it was my wife who was involved in the beauty.

She had skied for more than fifty years. The rhythm is in her bones, and the technique comes as naturally as the snow and mountains she has skied on. As one grows older, there seems to be a built-in time clock to promote caution, even hesitation. Longtime skiers think that maybe they shouldn't be trying to do what used to come so easily.

But not on this wonderful day last winter as I stood at the bottom of the trail, having felt my own need for the slower, premeditated pace. I looked up the open slope and saw Marion, with skis parallel, rhythmically gliding down through the powder snow as though years had fallen from her shoulders and air floated beneath her feet.

154

There is a time, even in retirement years, when if we let ourselves we may recapture some of the spirit and confidence of youth. We can outdo ourselves. Indelibly imprinted on my mind at any season will be the picture of green-clothed grace with which a woman shed a half-century of time and negotiated a white expanse of snow with more dancing lightness than I had ever seen her do before.

Is it in the body or is it in the mind that such moments are made possible? I know only that the word *retirement* can have its special moments when all that one has learned over the years can come together in a glorious experience, worth having, watching, and remembering forever.

Those whose bodies and minds have been conditioned over the years to a form of coordination — given good health — seem too often to neglect this possibility after retirement. It might be swimming, hiking, even weaving and rug-braiding, with walking worked in between the concentrated periods. It might be splitting wood leisurely or trimming hedges, or the even sweep of a paintbrush over the clapboards. It might be any of many forms of being active. To the extent we are able, we should reexplore what the mind and body have put together for us and we have allowed to slip into disuse.

One thinks back to earlier efforts that depended on strength and strength alone — like pushing the hay into the loft or pulling the plow guided by a young boy. One looks back to three times over the mountain in one day looking for deer — or getting the jeep out of an unexpected bog. These are incidents of strength, taken in stride because they were in tune with the fewer years that had preceded them.

In those retirement years, however, it is not strength but coordination that from time to time blossoms. It is called "timing" of the effort involved. It is a re-call of experience, a regeneration of confidence and skill.

Of such moments are born the ingredients in which skill again conquers a challenging ski trail with grace. Yet each of us in other challenges may again call up those deeply imbedded resources — a call to action based on experience.

To whatever degree it may be possible to seek these special moments in retirement, the effort — within a reasonable range of safety — should be made. Old does not mean ossified.

I Scream, You Scream . . .

I HAVE BEEN an ice-cream buff since childhood. As eight-year-olds, we kids used to sit in Wardwell's Ice Cream Parlor on white, filigreed metal chairs and dash our spoons into Wardwell's heavenly vanilla while chanting the familiar words of those days, "I scream, you scream — we all scream for ice cream."

The best, by far, I have ever tasted was when, during our honeymoon in Maine, Marion and I discovered the little store in Penobscot. In a glass dish (glass dishes are best for ice cream) was a high white pyramid filled with fresh peaches. It came from a large, hand-turned ice-cream freezer, and its main ingredient was cream so thick you could hardly push your finger into it.

This became the ultimate, against which Marion and I have tested many commercial brands during the years; we have compared it with that served in gourmet restaurants and have experienced disappointment after disappointment.

The other day I walked into Page's Ice Cream Stand on Brattleboro's Route 9. More specifically, I strolled out into the new addition where he makes the thirty-odd flavors for his retail stand, for wholesale, and for some of the best restaurants in the area. Doug Huntley and his wife, Irene, were busy at the ice-cream-mixing-and-freezing machine, a gleamingly neat metal unit that costs a small fortune. Doug looked up and asked, "How would you like a taste of something brand new?"

I got the taste buds on my tongue all set as he took a dish and held it to the opening of the machine from which he was filling two-gallon containers for his retail store. The ice cream that emerges from that spout is of the exact softness that ice cream should be for full appreciation of its taste. His wife snatches each container at the moment he fills it and rushes it into the large freezer, where it is held for twenty-four hours at twenty degrees below zero, and then takes some of it to his retail store where it is kept for twelve hours, "tempting" at seven degrees above zero.

I sampled a spoonful from the dish he had given me, just as it emerged from the machine. Man! It was the closest to that little Penobscot store that I have tasted in forty-nine years since then. I downed the rest of the dish and looked yearningly at the folds of it dropping from the machine into his container.

"Marvelous," I said. "But I don't recognize the taste."

"It is pure cream, with no other flavor," Doug replied. "It's something I thought I would experiment with." It seems that his basic recipes are the old-time ones he obtained from Floyd Page when he bought that business four years ago. "I've changed some for what I thought was improvement and have added a few of my own. The one you just tasted I list as 'Sweet Cream.'"

He uses nothing but pure flavors — extracts of coffee and maple, for instance — and fresh fruit. "The secret of quality ice cream," he said, "is measurement and weight. It must be exact to a gram. For example, vanilla ice cream from five gallons of cream uses exactly four ounces of vanilla flavor, and one-half gallon of ice cream must weigh at least thirty-six ounces, to satisfy federal regulations." He was running close to forty-one ounces while I was watching.

157

I think the thing that surprised me was the realization that he was using a thick cream, from the traditional farmer's milk and cream can. Because he adds no chemicals, his ice cream starts to break down after nine days — the water separating from the solids in the container. Commercial ice cream for grocery stores and supermarkets is loaded with chemicals to keep it for a month or more. It has to be because of distances and time involved in its delivery. The retail stores need protection against spoilage, and to give them time needed for selling. Page's does deliver to some retail stores, but those stores are willing to work within the nine-day limit in order to have quality.

When Doug said that he worked twenty hours on each of two days of the week, I asked, "What? Making ice cream?"

"No," he said. "I have another business besides this one. I deliver well-known Vermont dairy products to 1,400 customers around the country. My son, Doug Jr., delivers three days, and I deliver two in addition to my hours here."

Doug was in the trucking business before he went into ice cream. Before that, which explains his ease with recipes, weights, and measures, he spent three years as a chef at Dartmouth College. Pastry was his specialty, but when President Eisenhower visited Hanover, Doug was the chef who cooked his meal. At that same time, he cooked for the football team.

"A pound of meat for each player, three meals a day. Coach Blackman insisted," he said.

As I was leaving, I said that I noticed he was open early this spring, on some pretty cold days for ice cream.

His reply was, "One day I was waiting on a young fellow with my coat on. I told him I must look foolish serving ice cream in my parka."

"You don't look as foolish as I will," the customer replied, "standing out here eating it, shivering."

It Happened in Grasmere

IN THE SUMMER of 1932, a year after we were married, Marion and I boarded the *Britannic* in Boston for a trip to England. We were young and footloose, had both been English majors in college, and were eager to visit scenes related to British authors.

The tourist fare was within the means of my savings as a traveling book salesman, which had been augmented by some elasticity in expense-account items. And a thorough study of a guidebook of bed-and-breakfast plans convinced us that by relying on inexpensive lodging and bus travel we could swing it. We didn't realize then that our trip home would be in the steerage section of the old *Majestic*.

From Liverpool we started to work our way north to the Lake District. I shall remember Liverpool as the place where I was briefly introduced to the nature of British dentistry at that time. Whatever was applied to a tooth with a dying nerve proceeded for the next several days to eat the tissue away in my mouth.

But the pleasures of busing, walking and new people and places dimmed that slight problem until we reached Bristol. I shall remember Bristol as the place where I was introduced to small-town dentistry of those days in England. The pudgy gentleman, who moved around his district like an itinerant peddler, came to the bed-and-breakfast house, placed his bag of tools on the floor, reached a grimy hand into them, and tackled the nerve as I leaned back in the kitchen chair.

I felt fine after that, and we were in the beautiful Lake District, with its ever-present English showers bringing the greenest of green along the rolling hills, white-flecked by hundreds of sheep.

We were fascinated by Grasmere, a beautiful village surrounded by hills and possessing its own small lake, which can

159

be seen from the village streets. The poet William Wordsworth had lived here a couple of centuries ago with his talented sister, Dorothy. After spending some time at Dove Cottage, we visited the little graveyard behind Grasmere's ancient stone church where he was buried. When a heavy shower came, we took shelter in the church, sitting out the rain in one of the old pews.

This was in 1932. I shall leave our trip to England at that point and move to a scene in this Vermont house in the early 1960s.

The young man sitting in the chair on the other side of the room was a friend Mary Ann had met in classes at Harvard, and as fellow members of a rock-climbing group.

His accent was definitely English, and he was at graduate school at Harvard on a scholarship arranged by the British Labour Party.

"Peter's home is in Grasmere," Mary Ann said. "His father is the headmaster of the Grasmere School."

When Mary Ann completed her work in college and went to Africa on a volunteer teaching program, Peter still had another year at Harvard. He stayed with us on a number of weekends, and during the Christmas holiday he was at nearby Stratton Mountain learning to ski. He got a job in the Base Lodge kitchen and slept in the basement of the ski area church. I have a feeling that Mary Ann, who is an expert skier, had rather insisted that Peter learn how to handle a pair of skis. And he did.

It was shortly after Mary Ann's return from Tanzania, and Peter Hildrew's return to England, that she and Peter were married.

Thirty-five years after we had taken shelter from the rain and sat in a pew of the old Grasmere church, we returned to the church for their wedding.

It was a typical Church of England wedding, with the rector, in his black robe, fully in charge. But when the ceremony was completed and Peter's best friend at the old organ turned on all the knobs and swung into music full of exultation, the old church fairly quivered with the rhythm and beat of a talented young musician having himself a time.

When Mary Ann, Peter, Nicholas, and Eric left for home last week, after one of their none-too-frequent visits, we had enjoyed one more of the many happy experiences that — if nearly fifty years ago we had been able to see the future among the old beams of the Grasmere church — we might have anticipated long before any of them happened.

Where Did the Cream Go?

MY DAIRY FARMER FRIENDS will jump down my throat about this one. So hold your fire Herm, Charlie, Jack, Rick — I'm simply reminiscing about what happened to cream over the years. Milk cows are your business — reminiscing is mine. You deal with statistics, bureaucratic regulations, and the milk market. I'm not moving in that deeply on the cream factor, a subject you farmers could discuss in detail. I am only dealing here with the question of what happened to cream during my own life. There has been a drastic change in importance given to cream today as compared with sixty years ago. This is history, short and sweet.

After the cows had been milked, when I was a boy, my Aunt Doll (and I have never known whether that was her real name or not) used to put the milk in pans on a reasonably cool shelf where the cream came to the top and could be scooped off. Often I got caught sticking my finger into a pan and licking it.

I usually tried to know where Buttercup's pan was. Buttercup was pure Jersey, light tan with a darkish forehead and a bag full of cream.

I know it is heresy to bring up this point about a Jersey cow in the town where this is being written, which harbors the headquarters of the Holstein-Friesian Association of America. These Holsteins, the black-and-white cows so clearly identified around the world, are the top milk producers for today's market. They aren't expected to be big cream producers. They fit into our calorie-oriented society and have earned their top spot. There may be some of my dairy friends who believe differently, and probably could prove it. Who am I, an ink-stained newspaperman, to argue with them about udder things?

Anyhow, when we sat around the table as kids down in Maine, we expected cream on our oatmeal. Our father and mother expected cream in their coffee.

One can still buy a half-pint of cream—but for a pot of gold; this former cream-lapper now reaches for one of those admirably spouted paper cartons that scream out their contents in bold letters. "Skinny-You" or "Sleek Drink" or "Diet Milk" are the kind of warnings used to tell you they have spared your figure from coming in contact with that delicious topping of cream that used to loom so clearly in the glass bottles.

So I fill up my glass and offer you a toast to good health. What do I fill it with? Aunt Doll would have called it, with curled up lip, just what it is. She would have added, I am sure, "Skim milk, fit only for the pigs."

Sorry, Aunt Doll, I've learned to like it. I would feel, and look, more like a pig if I were still sticking my finger into Buttercup's cream.

I recall the day my father brought a gadget into the house that was to replace the spoon or tiny dipper used to remove the thick cream at the top of the bottle.

It was a device that was part cup and part moveable metal and used in a way that floated the cream off the milk, down to the last drop of sweetness. Not only were the cereals and coffee the gainers, but so also were strawberries, raspberries, blueberries and other fruits that seemed naked without a covering of thick cream.

Townspeople came to Aunt Doll's milk pantry for their bottles of milk, and they expected to see at least three inches of cream at the top. The price for a quart was seven or eight cents. Correct me if I am wrong, Herm. It may have been less.

Later, in Auburn, I worked weekends with a milkman, running along beside his horse-drawn sled to keep warm. He needed a helper on those days because he collected his money once a week. Cream was still in the good graces of the public — not separately but because it still was with the milk.

In the past thirty or forty years, the processing of milk in plants outside the farmers' individual operations has in itself brought changes in the relation of cream to milk. Bring in the cheese producers as part of the change.

There was a time, after health officers had come into the picture, when part of a health officer's job was inspecting restaurants to make sure the milk they were serving contained the legal minimum of butterfat. Was it four per cent?

The calorie story eventually got across to the public and the old salad days of cream were gone forever.

For the Birds

I'M NOT A BIRDWATCHER. Rather, I am a birdfeeder. Whereas I don't put out all the seed, I put out enough of it to take an interest in who eats it. My main concern is to see that enough intruders are kept away from the suet stations and the cylinder full of sunflower seeds to avoid unnecessary refills. I operate on the theory that bird feeding is for the birds, not for squirrels. So I am antagonistic toward squirrels that can get to the seeds in the feeders.

I have strung all kinds of contraptions on the lilac tree from which the squirrels leap to the hanging bird feeder. I seem only to have made their jumping easier. They use my wired contraptions just as a diver would to take a high dive to a small tub of water. Only the squirrels are more accurate. They land exactly on the rim of the cylinder holding the seed.

This requires quick reflexes on my part, for I have to slowly slide the glass door open, reach for the cord to the seed cylinder, and flip the squirrel ten feet into the air. I figure that for each ten feet I flip him it takes him ten minutes to recover his peace of mind and start heading for another try. The feud is never-ending, but I estimate that my efforts add about an extra day between refilling times on the sunflower cylinder.

As a feeder-watcher, I naturally see a lot of chickadees during the winter. Or do I see the same chickadees lots of times? They do look alike but vary in size, and they are as active as all get out, bouncing in with their swooping flying movement and bouncing out.

I recognize a tufted titmouse when I see him. The male and female hop around the ground and pick up what the clumsy chickadees have dropped. In this same way, this bird-feeder watcher recognizes sparrows — a grounded bird.

In a rural area like this, the raccoons are a problem on the suet feeders. They were scooping ours out until I wedged a weight down on top of the suet too heavy for them to dig out and toss away. It is a quarter of a pig of lead used on the old newspaper linotype machine and is heavy. It was a joy to throw a flashlight on a 'coon trying to dislodge this remnant of the pre-electronic-printing period.

As for the birds, there is a species that I believe is called pine siskins, wherever they got that name. They are without the slightest appreciation of what a bird-feed supplier is trying to do out of his own morning cereal budget. This stuff, bird feed, costs money and has to be budgeted. The pine siskins don't know this, and they peck away at the bird feeder, spitting out six seeds for the one small enough for them to handle. I sit and watch in disbelief. My dander rises, and I consider giving the whole humanitarian effort up. But then I remember the faithful chickadees—so constant, so appreciative, and relatively economical.

Yesterday the whole thing seemed worthwhile for a moment. We had dropped some thistle seed. To it came the bird of birds, the male cardinal—brilliant against the white snow, looking at us through his black mask, making a bird-feeding station a joy.

This morning two deer ate off the bottom limbs of the euonymus vine, fifteen feet away. Maybe we should open the doors and let everything that flies or walks come in the kitchen. "Scrambled eggs, youse guys?"

Old Swimming Holes

WHEN WE FIRST MOVED out to this rural road, and after our son was seven or eight, we built a swimming hole in the brook down front. We did it simply by damming it with rocks and wood.

The water came direct from Iceland. On a hot summer's day, however, a quick in and out seemed to do the trick.

Something about the human body eventually rebels at extreme cold, and we went looking nearby for warmer water. First we found a pool in the West River, sunny but still cold. Then we found a pool in the Williamsville Branch River, down a steep bank where we could get enough swimming in a fairly warm pool or go upstream and bask in the shallow and relatively warmer eddies of water. There also was the deep pool in

Stickney Brook, with steep walls for sliding.

Finally, we decided to have our own pool in the meadow above the house, where the sun stayed the longest. We could fill it by gravity from a couple of old wells. Our motivation and planning came during a period when the local economy was at an ebb and it was a buyer's market with builders. This was in 1958; but we were optimists.

We hired Pete Butinski to build a pool similar to one we had admired, which was the first filtered one in the area and now defunct. Pete had never built a swimming pool, which was good. It was good because he built it like the foundation of the Empire State Building—solid cement reinforced with steel rods. We couldn't look at such an endeavor for today's prices, but then we looked and said to go ahead.

Over the years we have merely had to paint it, which we could do ourselves and sometimes with the help of offspring or neighbors. We swim as a neighborhood.

Long ago the valve broke in the pipe that took the water from the bottom of the pool through the filter. So we improvised. We put a plug in the bottom of the pool, like in a bathtub. This has to be carefully snatched when we empty the pool in the fall, because the pool is built into the side of the meadow hill and has half of one wall above ground. We don't want to test ice pressure against that wall even though it is a foot thick. The plug has to be carefully pulled by a long pole to which we attached a hook. It sometimes takes half an hour to get the hook into the plug, a task that provides an annual lesson in patience. Good for the soul.

When the hillside pool is drained, we put the plug back in, this time with ropes through it. The pool thus receives enough rain and snow to make an insulating cushion for the bottom to rise and fall on its caulking as the frost exerts its pressure during the long winter.

Ah, that important caulking! This past fall, when it was filled to about four feet by rain and early snows, a muskrat got into it and ate long strips of the caulking in his effort to find a way out. He was probably paying me back for a column I wrote last year about my boyhood days of muskrat trapping. If so, I now promise the muskrat tribe never to say another thing about trapping. I don't ever want to be confronted again with the problem of finding a caulking that will bind with old industrial tar caulking, which Pete put in twenty years ago. There was a serious question as to whether the pool would ever again hold water.

It did, after we filled it a few weeks ago; it's filled now from the driven well near the house, through 200 feet of hoses. When we put that well in, and after it was obvious that gravity wells could no longer cope with modern appliances, we struck water at 150 feet; a geologist friend tells us that it must be a sizable underground stream. Its 25 gallons per minute still supplies the house during the 10 days we are pumping 20,000 gallons of water into the pool.

Now crystal clear, what is probably the oldest cement pool in the county still provides an opportunity for us to enjoy its therapeutical treatment, received merely by floating on our backs and soaking in the peaceful tree-lined meadow around us while contemplating the universe above.

This year, its twentieth, it not only will be a swimming hole for visiting grandchildren from Maine but also will sort of celebrate its survival by offering its pleasures to visiting grandchildren from England.

Doing the Dishes

IT WAS ONLY about ten years ago that I became involved in changing a newspaper from printing with metal to computerized production, which eliminated metal typesetting. This was my introduction to what thousands of little wires ca do to replace human hands and minds.

At the moment, I have an obsession about the possibility of a computerized dishwasher. Sit in the living room, press a button and the computer washes the dishes. An automatic dishwasher is almost that, but not quite.

As you can imagine, I have just finished a completely voluntary chore — doing the dishes. It is a daily, day-in and day-out, operation. Once you volunteer, you are a marked man.

For years I could escape, avoid, or disregard the fact that dishes have to be washed, at that time by hand. I had important things to do in connection with getting out a newspaper, didn't I? But then came retirement.

One of the things you face in retirement is the fact that you have more time, at least *some* more time, around the house. I began to see what my wife had been doing while I was occupied elsewhere. There is such a thing as fairness, so I volunteered on dishes — now that we had a belated automatic dishwasher — and inadvertently on a few other things.

It is dishwashing I am concerned with at this writing, because it is so relentless. I hadn't realized it. I now do.

Our dishwasher has stood up well, which I attribute partly to the fact that I can't bear to put a dirty dish in the dishwasher. I scrub 'em clean before doing my personally mathematical placing of them in the slots and spaces, so they will all go in. I wash even the tin cans so the raccoons won't dig them out of the plastic waste bags. By the time I push the button I feel that the job that should be done automatically has mostly been done by me. That's why I want a computerized process.

The fact is, I am in the Ph.D. stage of dishwashing. My introduction to this sloppy-handed side of life took place more than fifty years ago. I had acquired an athletic scholarship to

Andover, a prep school that recognized that sons of school-teachers couldn't afford its tuition, let alone its board.

The scholarship took care of the tuition, but I had to work for my board. I landed a job at the America House (where "America" was written), which was one of the eating houses for students. I didn't begin as dishwasher but was given the chance to work up to it. I was started as plate-cleaner — into a row of large cans — and was told that if I did well as a plate-cleaner I might become a dishwasher. These were washed by hand, of course — no automatics yet.

I made it. I became one of six dishwashers during the early part of the winter term. Further, by spring term I had been promoted from number one dishwasher (only the dessert dishes) to a waiter in the dining room where more affluent fellow students and some co-members of the track team sat on their posteriors without knowing what the America House kitchen looked like — which was not so good.

Later I graduated to selling neckties through the dormitories, which brought in enough money to pay for my meals. How would I fare in that job at today's prep schools?

Now, every time I hear the words of "America," written in that eating house by the Rev. Samuel Smith in 1832, I wipe my hands automatically on the front of my clothing where the white apron used to be, in the 1920s.

This brings me back to my sharing in the "women's and men's lib" of today. My wife cooks, I do dishes. In fact, my wife is not only a better writer than I am but a better painter of walls and ceilings. She has a long-handled paint roller moving across the ceiling above me right now, and not a drop is spilling on my head. She seems to like it, so I am not concerned about computerized painting — I'll settle for computerized dishwashing. The present automatic? The most automatic thing about it is that it happens every day.

Just what good is my Ph.D. in dishwashing going to do in these days, when Ph.D.'s are not automatically guaranteeing the opportunities they used to?

Mr. Gilfeather's Turnip

THE GILFEATHER TURNIP is a remarkable vegetable. It is also unknown outside the small corner of southern Vermont where it has produced for over a hundred years. It is a member of the mustard family and has the same small round seeds as the mustard plant.

Trouble is, you can't buy these seeds from a catalog or in displays of seed packages. It is necessary to be a friend of somebody in this area of Vermont who may give you a few seeds for your own garden. I know of only one farmer in the county who grows Gilfeather turnips commercially.

Years ago John Gilfeather, in the small town of Wardsboro, made a certain selection of seeds from his turnip crops and eventually came up with a turnip that is sweet and almost fluffy. A neighbor refers to this cooked dish as "angel feathers."

As everybody knows, the usual yellow turnip is not sweet. It is among the lowliest of vegetables, and few gardeners bother to grow it. One can see fields of turnips in European countries where such sturdy root vegetables are inexpensive but nourishing. There are no big fields of Gilfeathers. A few of them are grown for the local market, but mostly they are a home crop of a few plants — grown by those lucky enough to have been given some seeds.

Horace Winchester, of Brattleboro, who has raised Gilfeathers for twenty years, plants his seed about the fifteenth of June. First, a few rows are started, he says, to get the plants to seven inches. These are transplanted about a foot apart.

Around November, following cold days and a frost or two, they are harvested. After brushing and washing, they are strung up to dry. Finally, they are put in a Glad bag and tossed into the vegetable cellar.

The seeds of this kingly cousin to the rutabaga are easy for the grower to obtain from his own garden—if the grower possesses a large amount of patience. When the turnips are dug in the fall, leave a few in the ground. In the next spring, these plants will grow to about six feet. On each main stalk of treelike growth will be yellow blossoms. As these die, pods form that— when they turn yellow—are hung to get the pods thoroughly ripened. The pods should be cut into a basin where they are squeezed to get the seeds. This is where the patience comes in.

As I have said, the seeds of the Gilfeather are not generally available in the marketplace. I know of only one store that sells them. Bernard Putnam, proprietor of Brown and Roberts hardware store, had an oversupply of seeds in his own garden, so he's selling them at a nominal price. My wife obtained some from her hairdresser, who had been given them by a customer from Dover. They looked very much like poppy seeds.

A while later she gave our daughter from England some poppy seeds. In due time our daughter wrote, "The poppies are up but please tell me why they look like turnip plants?" She was unaware of the mix-up of seeds and threw the plants away. There could have been a foothold in England for the Gilfeather turnip.

As I sat the other day with Horace Winchester and his wife, sharing our admiration for Mr. Gilfeather's invention so many years ago, I thought what a typical Vermont native Horace is. Tall, spare, firm lips, economical in the use of words, he certainly comes from generations of Vermonters. Not so. He was born in London and went to school in Scotland and Canada. He was a young man when he arrived in Brattleboro, where for forty years he was to be office and personnel manager of the Holstein Association, the large registering complex for the black-and-white cows all over the world.

At eighty-five, Horace gives seeds to friends, as he has been doing for years, a sort of Johnny Turnipseed. And his wife, who has cooked many a turnip, has good advice on cooking a Gilfeather.

"Cut it up in thin slices. You may have to use a hammer as well as a knife. Boil thirty minutes. Put through a ricer. Add butter, salt and pepper. And never have a New England boiled dinner without Gilfeather!"

If this has whetted your appetite, you simply will have to take my word for this vegetable's sweetness. We fortunate people are pretty much confined to this little section of New England.

Sorry about that.

Little Skis: Big Castle

MARIUS (LODI) LODEESEN, a Dutch pilot for Pan Am, turned on the automatic switch that steers the plane safely for the next thousand miles and settled back in his seat. He reached into the bag beside him and pulled out a paperback book.

This was in the fall of 1958.

He had read *Instant Skiing* by Clif Taylor a dozen times already. But he wanted to get the rhythmic turns fixed in his head because in a few weeks, at age fifty-seven, he would start teaching himself to ski on one of the Austrian Alps. He would be retiring in a few years, and he was determined that skiing would be one of his pleasures in the coming years of leisure.

Three years later, he not only had learned to ski on his three-foot Taylor-made Shortee-Skis, but to ski well. Further,

172

he had become a short ski addict and spent considerable time trying to persuade others to take up skiing on "the little ones."

It was in that third year, when he was skiing on his favorite Alp, that he suddenly saw a woman lying in the snow beside the trail. Her long skis were crossed under her. She was crying.

"I can't handle these skis," she told Lodi as he bent over her.

Lodi helped her get down to the base lodge at the foot of the mountain. Later, over a cup of tea, he asked her if she wouldn't like to have him get her a pair of three-foot skis and teach her how to use them. She accepted his offer and they skied together for the next week or so.

One day she invited Lodi to her home in Germany. Lodi's eyes opened wide when he saw her home.

It was the castle Schweinsberg, on a high hill, where it had been for 700 years. Surrounded by walls and ramparts, it still contained the ancient guns with which it had been defended. Beneath its 45 rooms were the dungeons that contained the bones of prisoners who had been thrown into the dungeons centuries ago.

Lodi recovered from that surprise only to learn that his friend was Baroness Von Schweinsberg. But she now was also a master of the three-foot ski, the prime symbol by which Lodi judges the attractiveness and intelligence of people.

After their return to the Austrian Alps, they decided to get married. Lodi's skis then led to his new home — in a castle.

They led also, just the other day, to Clif and Mary Taylor's — where Marion and I had been invited to meet him. We arrived just ahead of the Lodeesens, who also brought their Hanover, N.H., hosts because they were also interested in hearing Clif's latest ideas on the art of teaching nonskiing adults how to enjoy wending their way down a snow-covered mountain.

Lodi is slight and wiry, with twinkling eyes shining over his

white moustache and goatee. It is hard to believe that Clif had told me this man was seventy-six years old.

With a baroness aboard, Mary Taylor had put a few extra touches on a lunch that surrounded a delicious German potato salad. Marion, knowing that an extra dish always helps when there are several to feed, had whipped up a lobster salad with homemade mayonnaise.

When it turned out that all eight of us at Clif's house were devotees of the short ski—and knowing that it was Clif who invented the original "Shortee Ski"—we figured we were sharing a sort of anniversary, a sort of "Short-Ski Festival."

Lodi asked, "May I play my 'Shortee-Ski song'?" He then stood up, pulled a harmonica out of his pocket, and went into fast-beat music with a Bavarian rhythm.

Suddenly, he stopped playing the harmonica and sang his song, which started with words like these:

> *Clif Taylor's skis are short and sweet,*
> *A nicer ski you'll never meet.*
> *A slide and flutter down the mountain,*
> *Like water slipping from a fountain.*

Lodi laughed, and his white goatee bobbed with excitement. "Skiing is a way of life," he said. "When you are our age, live it up—on short skis."

You never know when you will find your castle!

Right to Be Alone

LONELINESS IS NOT something to be sought after. It is a form of deep deprivation. One is lonely when he is deprived of the presence of someone he cherishes, or even of those for

175

whom he has only a fondness amounting to pleasure of their company. The longer the deprivation and the deeper the affection, the greater the sense of loneliness.

Yet, one can cherish being alone, when there is the privilege of choice, And in that sense not enough people have the privilege these days to be alone, or the opportunity or the initiative to seize the opportunity when it is available. In a crowded world where gregariousness and group activity and collective effort press in on the individual, solitude is hard to come by.

But not so in rural America. One of the virtues of country living is the opportunity to still find solitude when one needs it.

It is my guess that not all fishermen go to the brooks and streams primarily in search of fish, nor all hunters to the woods looking for deer, nor even all joggers to the back roads to strengthen their cardiac muscles. Fish and game and healthy exercise can be the main motive, but they can also be sidelines. The main motive can be, and quite justifiably so, a desire to be alone, to think inwardly in solitude, to shake out the cobwebs that are spun by the problems of life's complexities.

Sometimes just sitting on an old stone wall surrounded by hemlocks does it, or a walk along an old logging road. On such occasions the mind slows to a sluggish stop, then starts to beat with the slow rhythm of winds in the trees, the eternal murmuring of a brook, or the silent curling of smoke from a distant chimney. In this relaxed fashion the mind searches out pleasant memories or awakens to submerged hopes. It comes alive in an awareness of one's self. If the youth of today think they discovered the question "Who am I?" they simply haven't lived long enough to know for how many centuries and by how many numbers of people of all ages this search for identity has been going on—and going on when others least suspect it.

Don't let the fact that the man appears to be fishing fool you. Don't underestimate the soul-searching of the hunter seated on the log, or the berry-picker whose head is hardly discernible above the blackberry bushes halfway up the mountain.

The right to be alone is an inalienable one, and it must be exercised to be appreciated. This is not to say that the right of communal action through the democratic process is to be treated lightly. It is not to say that togetherness, brotherly love, neighborliness, and sense of community should not be nurtured and improved.

It is simply to say that there are times when it is as good as it is necessary to be alone. After all, society begins with the individual. He ought to take a walk with himself once in a while to become reacquainted. It can't do any harm — and it might do some good.

Nicholas Discovers America

RETIREMENT HAS A WAY of building its own routine. It has been a long time since we were involved in the activities of children. We concentrate on our own activities, our own routine. We are no longer surrounded by children's laughter, even though we sometimes seem to hear it in the quiet house.

Suddenly the house is full of children again. Routine gives way to an excited child's voice. The laughter is real and contagious. The immediate world around us is again seen through the eyes of a child, in this case through the eyes of a four-year-old English grandson for whom this meadow, the stone walls, and the climbing ledges are a new world.

An ocean separates him from his home. Yet he is at home here, the home his mother grew up in and he and his baby brother Eric are visiting. He even knows just what he wants to see here, because his grandmother had written stories to be read to him during the past year.

He knew there are raccoons here and could imagine just what they look like, even though there are none in England. He wanted to see the chipmunks, which don't exist in England. He was not excited about seeing familiar fireworks when he could at last see the unfamiliar fireflies whose brilliant sparkle lights up a dark New England night.

As you may appreciate, Nicholas was not concerned with the differences we older ones know distinguish England from the United States. Why should we try to explain the difference in size between the two countries, or how once the country we live in was part of England, or even how far he had flown to get here? The world of Nicholas is what he sees with his own eyes. Why should we comment on the fact we speak the same language with different pronunciation. Nicholas knows what he wants to say and how he chooses to say it.

It is his four-year-old world that we are permitted to enter and to share. It is a revitalizing experience seen through the eyes of a small boy.

There are two sides to this world a four-year-old creates for himself, the make-believe and the real. This doesn't have to be enough for us. It is enough for him, and he can live them separately or together. It is hard to say which he is living when he dons his knapsack, puts a few of his father's discarded bits and pieces of climbing gear around his neck and announces, "I am going rock climbing."

He tackles the ledges behind the house with his sturdy legs, ledges that really don't rise very steeply. He peers through his blue eyes at each tiny crevice, seeking a good handhold. And one can observe the blond hair on his head move from side to side as he slowly climbs what to him is doubtless a steep and challenging slab of sheer rock — the kind he has seen climbers on during the rock-climbing holidays his parents have taken him on where he could stand at the bottom of the cliff watching.

This time, however, he is climbing his own cliff.

This is his make-believe world. The high point of his real world was when he saw his first raccoon. This was on an evening when his parents had put out some chicken-meat bait to lure the raccoon to the back porch, where he could be seen through the sliding glass door. It was an evening of waiting. For the parents, it required patience. For Nicholas, determination was enough. He knew the raccoon would come, and when he did there was that happy shout of delight. "Look," he said, "it has hands and fingers to pick the food out of the jar." This is discovery.

On another day, when he came running through the door to tell his mother there was a chipmunk in the stone wall, it was another discovery — not story-book, but real. It had to be seen to be his, and it will stay with him because nobody has to tell him there are chipmunks in America. He now knows there are.

The rapture of watching his first fireflies doesn't require an adult explanation of how the insects produce their lights. The mystery is enough.

These experiences are what a four-year-old will tell his nursery-school classmates about. He went to America to see the animals his grandmother had written about, and he saw them with his own eyes.

A Day with Eric

WE HAD VOLUNTEERED to take care of our year-old grandson for a day while his parents got a break in their holiday visit. We had raised three of them, hadn't we? What could be so difficult about tending to the wants and needs of this baby, for just one day?

Even in a house that was strange to him he seemed happy

and contented when in the care of his parents. This was his first visit here, for the distance from England is not exactly one that can be covered frequently.

Our day alone with Eric had started off easily enough, as we took over at the time he was put down for his morning nap. This would give us a rested baby with which to start our tour of duty. We sat, with folded hands, wondered when the awakening summons would put to the test what we had remembered about babies, and what we hadn't.

The call came, good and loud. I got the privilege of going upstairs to fetch the grandson. As I stood over his crib, suddenly faced with the realization that he probably would need changing, the expression on his face seemed almost to be one of pity. I had the feeling that *he* was in charge, not me. The fact that he was so cheerful appeared ominous, as though he were saying, "What are you waiting for? Get on with it."

I plucked him from his crib, and while he took a tight hold on my hearing aid I got him and myself safely downstairs. I had a feeling he didn't need to be changed right then, or so I told myself.

In the meantime, my wife had been busy heating Eric's lunch.

"It's some horrible prepared stuff called turkey-and-rice. I hope it tastes better to him." She had stuck the tip of her little finger in to make sure it wasn't too hot, and curiosity about today's baby foods got the best of her. It turned out that Eric loved the stuff, and we were still moving along smoothly.

Then came the first major test. This time he did need changing.

It had all seemed so easy when our daughter or son-in-law did it, just as it had been easy for us, many years ago. In those days, diapers were diapers and folding them was an art. Since then progress has taken over with prefolded throwaways that don't require the safety pins that occasionally caught a finger.

I was kneeling on one side of Eric, Marion on the other. She nodded, and together we stripped the old off and reached for the new. Eric took it in stride, probably struck cryless by the amazing technique he was witnessing. His composure melted, however, when I fumbled with the piece of tape that has to come off to get to the sticky part that replaces the safety pin. I was all thumbs until she reached around from her side and hitched my side of the contraption.

"Well done!" I shouted, and we were free to plunge into the entertainment hours.

After exhausting the supply of toys, not to mention ourselves and possibly Eric, we decided it was such a nice day that a ride in the stroller was in order. It might calm us all down a bit. The stroller was one of those collapsible things that looks like a large folded umbrella. How to open it? Finally, I found the gadget, and we were off for a stroll.

I maneuvered the four little wheels up the incline to the path behind the barn, the longest stretch of flat ground on our hillside. After making the trip through the overhanging alders several times, I decided I had pushed far enough. That wasn't what Eric thought, however, and he let us know it. So, back into the stroller and some more huffing and puffing over the uneven terrain with a quiet baby who apparently was entranced by this unusual journey back and forth through the trees.

Everything went smoothly through supper, as did even the bath in the big tub, both of us getting almost as wet as Eric. We ended the day as we had started it, with a sleeping baby.

If I were asked what single word best describes baby care, I should have to answer, "constant." I don't know how parents ever meet this responsibility with the calmness that they do. I don't know how we did, as parents.

Sounds as Memory

THIS HOUSE HAS BEEN filled with some new sounds these past two weeks. They are particularly English sounds, as I am sure you would agree if you had been listening to these two small English grandchildren chattering away.

It is not for me to say that they don't speak clearly. I find that a hearing aid is inadequate for picking up the voices of children, in any language. But I find it a bit more difficult when a child is speaking English the way the English speak it.

Their father, Peter, has depth and roundness in his voice that fits his accent into the hearing aid very nicely. And whereas Mary Ann's way of speaking has not changed much during the fourteen years she has lived in England, it is a different tonal arrangement than when she was here as a girl. Rather nice, too.

But there have been new sounds within these walls. So, I was surprised when this evening took a turnabout and produced some older sounds, older and different from those Marion and I are used to. The kids had been put to bed, and Mary Ann was rummaging around in a cupboard for something that was especially interesting to her when she was a girl. I dropped my newspaper as I suddenly heard that ancient fox trot "Row, Row, Rosie" filling the room with the bouncing music I had first listened to as a boy up in Castine, Maine. She had found the tapes we had made of those old Victor Records that my family had given me when they sold the camp at Castine. We later turned the records over to Steve after they had been taped, and we have played only a few of them in the years since Mary Ann used to pull them out because she liked them, and still does.

One after another, the popular songs of fifty and sixty years ago took me back to my own boyhood—"Indian Love Call,"

"Rock-a-Bye Moon," "Don't Be a Fool, You Fool," "Knee Deep in Daisies," "Say, Arabella," "Swanee River Blues," "Cecelia," and a dozen more.

The sounds I was hearing, along with the music of the early twenties were from an old box victrola at the Castine cottage. There was the sound of the wind flapping the big curtains on the sleeping porch, the sound of clams being fried in the kitchen, the sounds of children being just as active as Eric and Nicholas have been around here today, many of them the sounds of children on a vacation just as the two grandchildren are.

They were old sounds. Those of my two English grandchildren are new.

KNEE DEEP IN DAISIES — OH YES

Steve, who came on from Chicago to share Mary Ann's and Peter's visit — and they found some skiing — says that the old records now at his house are still in perfect condition.

Country music is picking up these old pieces, as did Willie Nelson and his 1980 recording of "Blue Skies."

After finishing with "Poor Papa," sung by Jack Smith the "Whispering Baritone," Steve dug out a few of Victor Borge's records, guaranteed to produce a laugh from any listener. Why, I don't always know. For instance, as Borge told the bit from his "autobiography" — "My uncle asked how old I was. 'I'm five,' I replied. 'You ought to be ashamed,' he said. 'When I was your age I was ten.'" — well, I was laughing as I did years ago — and as son John did at age eleven when I took him to a Borge show in Washington. The blasting laugh he still has shook the audience almost as much as Borge did.

And so to bed, ready for another day and those new sounds around the house.

Facing the Rain

RAIN DOES THINGS to people. More than a little can be learned about a person's attitude toward life by the way he or she reacts to rain. The best place to indulge in this kind of character reading is in the rural areas of the north country. Rain in the city is a nuisance, yet it can be avoided with relative ease because of the many kinds of dry transportation available. In the country it has to be lived with. So it is in the country that rain does things to people, to the way they act and to how they face it.

The man who takes the rain full in the face and goes about his business has adjusted to the vicissitudes of daily living. Weather is weather to him, and except for accommodating his body and feet to water-shedding garments, he moves about in the same upright position as on sunny days.

It is the hunched ones who find a difference and show it. Their pace may be faster, but their accomplishments are fewer. They practice a process of elimination, leaving some things undone because the rain seems to interfere. On this fourth successive day of rain I guess I am one of those trying to keep out of that classification.

Some people enjoy taking a walk in the rain — not only because it gives them a feeling of being a part of their environment, but because they like what they see in the wetness of leaves and rivulets of water in the path. They are akin to those who prefer to fish in the rain, not only because the fish bite better but also because they, too, like to be out in that kind of weather.

One can excuse the females who emerge from the hairdressers when the rain is pelting hard. Some of them under ordinary circumstances may be rain enthusiasts, but with a new hair-do their enthusiasm has vanished.

The males who emerge from their coffee break and dash along Main Street with their collars up, from doorway to doorway, are rationalizers. They would have you think they can take any kind of weather in stride — no raincoats or umbrellas for them, that's kids' stuff. But look at them scamper, like so many squirrels. The fact is that they are oriented toward the dry and cozy indoors — the store, office, or home.

One has to make certain physical adjustments to weather, mostly in the way of adequate clothing. But weather does call for mental adjustments. It is not a case whether one is for it or agin it. The question is: is he with it.

I react to rain differently from the ways I used to. There was a time when I couldn't wait to get to a good trout brook in a heavy drizzle, knowing that no matter what I had on I would be wet to the gills when I got home. I have been a walker in the rain, and still do at times. But there is something about the way the years climb onto your back that make indoor chores a little more attractive when the rain has engulfed the woods and meadows. That's not to say that I really enjoy pushing the vacuum cleaner just because it is dry inside.

I do miss one challenge that rain offered, back when we would have a field of hay on the ground, sitting in windrows ready for loading onto the rack we had built over the jeep. On those occasions when black clouds would begin to appear on the horizon and calculations of time were in order if we were to beat the rain, there was indeed a challenge. There aren't many satisfactions greater than getting the last load into the haymow before the shower roared in.

One of the reactions to rain that I admire most is that of today's young people, especially the young who have chosen to live in, or be college-educated in, this nonmetropolitan section of the country. They not only face the rain, they lift their faces to it. They seem to find a fresh, healthy cleanness in it. Maybe it is because it blots out much of the ugliness hidden behind the sheaths of rain and low-hanging mists. It is the clean, washed, fresh world they are seeking.

The environment includes all kinds of weather. In this world at its best there is no bad weather — it is a matter of attitudes. An increasing number of young people seem to have found the openness of spirit that reaches into any weather.

Rain does things to people, and some of those things are good.

Lobsters from Utah?

A NEWS ARTICLE in the *New York Times* the other day

described the plans of two young researchers who "hope to raise lobsters in Utah."

This is the kind of news that shakes me. I have become accustomed to the headlines on international acts of violence, on the political chicanery of taking school lunches away from poor children, on crime, sex, and even on how compassionate is the government of South Africa.

But raising lobsters in Utah?

It seems that two researchers at Brigham Young University have spent seven years "breeding, hatching, studying and coddling lobsters" in the university's aquatic ecology laboratory. They claim success and now want to go into the lobster business commercially. They plan to build a solar-heated lobster ranch, utilizing Utah's hot sun and their knowledge of the right dry food and artificial salt water.

Even in his greatest dreams Brigham Young certainly didn't visualize lobster raising when he led his followers down to the Great Salt Lake. But two young researchers in the university have their own dreams—not in Salt Lake, because it is nine times saltier than the ocean, but in their solar-heated lobster ranch.

But commercially? Competing with Maine lobsters?

"Our lobsters taste just as good as the ocean versions," the researchers claim.

Now, here is the crux of the whole matter. It has been proved that lobsters can be raised in Utah, that they can be raised in twenty-one months as compared with an ocean lobster requiring seven years to reach the weight of one pound. But "tasting as good as ocean lobsters" is a claim raising serious questions.

What in Utah can be substituted for the smell of salty wood that entraps the lobster at the bottom of the ocean and permeates his very being? What aromas of the lobster boat, reeking with ocean smells, can soak into a lobster raised under a desert sun?

There can be no laboratory talk in a Utah laboratory that can match the living atmosphere of a Maine coast dock, where in the foggy, sunless hours before dawn the fishermen put their Downeast accents on every lobster trap, buoy, and gear that will rub off on every lobster caught that morning.

The smell of rubber boots and jackets, of fishermen's hands dunked in ocean waters for many years, of salt-encrusted boat planking—these go to the market with ocean lobsters, especially those caught off the shores of Maine. Where around the "solar-heated lobster ranch" in Utah can these ingredients of an ocean lobster be captured?

There is more to a lobster than taste, more than just what touches the tongue. There is an ocean atmosphere that embellishes the taste. It reaches the eyes through visions of lobstermen steering their boats in all kinds of weather. It reaches the nostrils through the aroma of salt air pushing through banks of fog.

The ocean lobster, wherever it goes, carries with it the lifestyle of its growing up. It is a reminder of the place from which it came and of the lobstermen who pulled their traps. And this is a part of how a lobster tastes.

And what about the tomalley—that luscious lobster liver that turns to ocean green when cooked and is the very essence of all that sun and sea have done to create a lobster? I cannot imagine a "solar-heated lobster ranch" doing justice to such a delicacy. They may look like lobsters in Utah. But taste like lobsters from Maine?

It is the sea that does it. As my father used to say when he raised his glass of clam water to toast us over our steamers: "Nectar of the ocean. Pride of the sea. Good enough for you. And good enough for me."

At Home with Art

It was still dark at 7:15 this morning. The clouds were heavy and low. A cold, fine snow filled the air, and four inches of it covered the ground with stillness. No day to be out and about, if you didn't have to. How warm and comfortable the house felt. An oasis in a white desert.

I lay there staring at the ceiling. Would this be a good day to paint out the gray area around the chimney left from repairing the roof leak months ago? I had become used to it. Rather liked the familiar sight each waking morning. Might as well leave it alone for a while.

This could be a day just to get up and enjoy the house as it is, to relish its isolating comfort, to forget any need for seeing people, to be content that within these four walls are more than forty years of accumulated experiences. And yet the forbidding nature of the outdoors this morning gave me the feeling of discovery, as if I were awakening for the first time to the pleasure of not having to do a single thing except enjoy the seclusion of this house.

As I started to turn on the TV just to glimpse the kind of world it might be beyond the enclosing horizons of the storm, I looked up at Robert Rondeau's painting of an ocean breaker bursting onto the beach at Popham. It refreshed me with its news of summers thirty years ago, when Marion and I and the three children dived excitedly into the breakers at Popham, pushing ourselves back onto the beach with laughter and fun.

I turned to look at Charles Pont's watercolor of this house, painted on a snow-filled winter day just after we had bought the old farm and before it had been given the benefits of electricity and central heating within a rebuilt interior. Charlie's picture, day in and day out, still continues to be that wonderful bundle of hope this old house was forty-two years ago.

189

During the course of today, intermingled with poking around in household odd jobs, I have made a day of visiting with the paintings, drawings, and photographs that liven the walls, each with a significant relation to our family experiences — from Steve's photographs of flowering dogwood, as fresh and moist as on the day he captured it, to the two paintings submitted by artists in 1942 for my children's book *Johnny-Jump-Up*. Each is a painting of a boy in a buckboard driving two lively horses on the story's route to Bucksport to get Castine's daily mail. The boy has his origin in my father's childhood experience on which the story is based — some hundred years ago. They glow with the salty sunshine and horsey exuberance of a long-gone period in American life.

On the mantle over the fireplace is a tiny watercolor by Mary Ann of the lake near Grasmere, England, softly British in its Lake Country setting and a daily association for us with Mary Ann's new home and our own visits to that corner of England. In the den is an old drawing of Cartmel, England, the quaint little village outside of which Mary Ann's father- and mother-in-law live, in their 17th-century stone farmhouse surrounded by gardens and fruit trees and flowers.

Also on the den wall is Grandfather Hooper's own drawing of his five-seater buckboard he drew to hang in the livery stable to advertise his offering of drives to the British campgrounds in Castine. Here are 150 years of pictorial history from the paintbrush of William Hooper around the year 1850.

And one we scarcely saw at all, it is so familiar at all times, is the dining room wall, covered entirely by an enlarged photograph taken by our friends the Snivelys in 1939 when we moved into the house. They shot this picture from the top of Bear Hill behind us, straight down to the valley of our neighbors. No finer valley there is.

The day inside this house has been vibrant with the events

190

that have sprung back into focus from paintings and photographs on its walls.

It has been a day full of years.

Sounds in the Night

MANY PEOPLE LIVE in places where certain sounds accompany the night and to which they become so accustomed that being away from them creates an uneasy difference. We once had a Fresh Air Fund child staying with us who was so used to going to sleep while a New York elevated train passed close by that he was alarmed by the silence that encompassed this country house at night. "I can't get to sleep in all this quiet," he would complain.

During my childhood on the Maine coast there were sounds in the night that became an important part of going to sleep. The canvas curtains on the screened porch were hung there to keep the rain out, but in the slightest wind they flapped with a sound like sails on a schooner. The harder it blew the more they flapped, and it didn't take a great deal of imagination to feel that you were far out at sea under full sail and the ship was gently rocking you to sleep.

It is the continuity of night sounds, I suppose, that weaves them into people's lives. Of such is the brook that not only flows beside the road a hundred feet below us but also flows through us. The part of the brook that permeates the members of this family is its sound, the never-ceasing sound to which we have listened for some forty years and that has been heard by the family offspring from the time they opened their ears to sound. It is that much a part of our lives.

On those occasions when city dwellers have stayed in this house their first reaction to separation from urban noises, the kind that interrupt sleep, is, "How quiet this place is." But in the morning, after having become accustomed to a noiseless night, their question is, "What was that sound, that murmuring roar that seemed to rise and fall as I lay there listening?" That was the sound of the brook.

After one has lived with it many seasons, through the spring freshets and the summer droughts, its tones and its infinite degrees of volume take on the fascination of constant discovery. A person may be one of many faces, but a brook's many faces are multiplied much beyond its visual appearance by the infinite variety of tongues it speaks.

From those peaks of frenzy, when its high water and its churning boulders have shouted the warning of larger floods downstream, to those deeply quiet summer nights when only the brook's murmur breaks the silence, the brook is indeed a garrulous babbler of good and bad tidings. It is never, itself, silent.

And this is why it has become part of us, a component of our physical and emotional vibration, an alerter and a soother, a guide to the eternal existence of beauty and a strong thread of continuity in the passage of days and years.

Quite apart from the effect of the brook's sound on our lives, a presence we miss when separated from it for any length of time, is the memory of pleasures it has given in helping bring up three children. A brook help raise children? Indeed, yes. In answer to that growing-up question, "What can I do now?" there was always the brook, like an English nanny, waiting to take the children in hand with an ample assortment of things to do—fishing, picking jack-in-the-pulpits, building dams—you name it. A brook can be a mother's helper to children for hours at a time.

For some years the brook played a part in the lives of other children, set aside by adjacent property owners for a mile or so as a "children's fishing brook." Stocked each year by Sports-men, Inc., it had the special role of introducing boys and girls (and frequently their parents) to what a clean brook in a deep valley has to offer with the joys of learning to fish. From where we sat, the sound of joyous young voices added to the familiar sound of the brook itself.

It not only has run past this house for many years; it has also run through us. It is the barometer of our inner weather. On those moments when we suddenly realize we are not hearing the brook at night, we know it is because we have let troubled thoughts block it off. We listen to it, and, in listening, we relax.

Nature Captured in Memory

FOR THE PAST HALF HOUR, a ruby throated humming-bird has been sitting on a line of thin rope outside my window. It is the line that leads from our back door, and it is used to lower the bird feeder when it needs refilling. There is an over-hang of the house above it, so the rope is dry and unaffected by the heavy rain falling just a foot away from it.

Never before have I seen a hummingbird sitting less than a few feet away. He is obviously drying his feathers, before going back to seek nectar in the drenching downpour.

I am no birdwatcher, but to have the utter surprise of watching this hummingbird, to study him from his long beak to tail, is a fascinating surprise. He is so much more bird than I ever thought the darting little creature could be, I can hardly believe my eyes.

What I have always seen was a tiny set of whirring wings that were more of a whir than they were wings. Now I see a tiny, three-inch bird preening like any other bird, shaking the water from real wings and ruffling its feathers.

This has been one of nature's greatest surprises for me. It also brings to mind that over the years it has been nature that has provided the surprises that linger in one's mind. The unexpected moments have been far between. They add up, now that I start to string them together, into a cluster of rare moments.

As I continue to watch the unusual sight of a quiet hummingbird, I think of some of the other surprises nature has offered. Each of them is a kind of thrill that no artificial, or man-made, experience could provide. Being surprised by the unexpected sight of some wild creatures in the quiet of natural surroundings is unlike any other thrill.

The first sight of a doe and new fawn in the meadow, seen through this same Vermont window, was no less exciting than seeing one's first bull moose in the midst of Maine's wilderness.

I was only a youngster walking from the fishing camp where I worked, when just on the other side of the stream I was approaching stood the big bull moose. It was at this same camp, in Maine logging country, that I rounded an abandoned bunkhouse to see my first bear. He was so busy, and I was so stricken with the unexpected nearness, that he finally walked away while I stood rooted.

Probably the most beautiful surprise nature has presented to me was the sudden appearance of a buck deer standing at the top of a Vermont hill while I stared at his enormous antlers against the background of a full moon.

There have been many others—first encounters with wildlife, some of which have been repeated over the rural years. Coons at my back door at night are a common sight now—but they were certainly a surprise to my ten-year-old grandson from Maine. He has started having his own series of what nature can do in the way of thrills that even TV can't provide for a little boy.

He, too, will probably have his first look at baby foxes playing in front of their den. He, too, may be sitting on a stone wall and suddenly see a bobcat sitting on the same wall. He, too, will have his first golden moment of a salmon leaping at the end of his fishing line.

My own son has already shown these two Maine grandsons where their father's exciting "firsts" took place here in Vermont. Just as pressed flowers in the sealed plexiglass preserve the beauty of nature, at the hands of modern craftsmen, the mind preserves experiences.

The sitting hummingbird outside the window, this rainy day, is now added to my collection of nature's rare moments. Have you had occasion, or such motivation, to run back over your own collection lately?

Above the Crowd

BEING PUT OUT TO PASTURE in old age is not in itself an uncomfortable situation, assuming that you can still move around and graze a bit. It helps, however, if one acquires the pasture philosophy rather early in life.

There is something about a pasture, any pasture, that separates it from the pressures of daily routine. It surrounds one with space, is quiet, and offers an interesting variety in the changes of weather. It also contains surprises and mysteries, ample opportunities to sit and think, and the pleasures of exercise when the mood is in that direction.

As far back as I can remember, especially in those early years of school, June meant packing up for the train and steamer trip to Penobscot Bay, where we would spend the summer with the ocean lapping the front steps and acres of pasture land spreading in back of us.

At the camp in Castine that father had built for our family to spend the long summer vacation, after he had turned the key in the principal's office at Webster Grammar School in Auburn, the place where we boys spent much of our time was Uncle Warren's pasture. Here were the raspberries and blueberries, caves in the ledges and long, narrow paths in the alders, and the cows to round up and drive to the barn every afternoon. It was a world in itself and a happy place.

After being out of pastures in the workaday world for several years, I met a man who spent a great deal of his time in and around pastures, not as a farmer but as a horse dealer. Of course, his urge was that he was fond of horses, so that buying and selling them took him the length and breadth of the state looking at pastures.

When I met Sanford Smith he had the Ford franchise in town. A lot of horse people became car dealers when livery stables gave way to garages. But Sanford didn't stay in the automobile business long, and among the activities he returned to was raising and selling riding horses.

I was no longer selling him automobile advertising at the newspaper, but, being a horsey person myself, I accepted journeys with him now and then to look at horses, and pastures.

A typical junket would be when he was taking a horse to pasture in his trailer and wanted to look at other horses he was thinking of buying for trading purposes. After putting his Welch stallion in an old Guilford pasture that had seen nibbling animals ever since 1791, we would go on toward Halifax, from pasture to pasture.

Here would come a golden mare as Sanford whistled at the gate, and at another a gray mare and colt would trot toward the gate for sugar. "How are you, girls? Just wanted to see how you were doing?" Sanford would say.

Among the journeys were trips to the great Morgan Horse

pastures of Woodstock and down to the huge stable to see Upway King Peavine, a champion American saddle stallion. Sanford usually had a mare along in the trailer to spend a few days with Mr. Peavine.

When we moved out here in the country, Sanford sold me my first horse, a retired racing mare, a pacer, named Reel. She had never been ridden, just pulled a sulky on the half-mile tracks in 2:18. "She'll make a good saddle horse," Sanford said. And she did, one that could be ridden for miles easily because of her being a pacer instead of a trotter, a nice ambling gait. She was our first horse in the pasture up back, the pasture that now has neither horses nor cows, just me.

But if you think it isn't still an attractive pasture, rising some 600 feet and 50 acres to the top of the hill, you should ask my sons and daughters what they do first when they arrive for a visit here on Sunset Lake Road.

Up through the pasture to the top of the hill they go, maybe reliving some of their experiences as kids, looking here and there to see if some of the trinkets they hid years ago are still here.

With Mary Ann and Peter, summer or winter and fresh in from England, the climb through the pasture repeats their weekly walks in the convoluting fells of the English Lake District.

Sitting here on top of the hill right now, I feel as I always did in a pasture — high above the crowd, sequestered in peace, yet in touch with the world.

CHRISTIAN HERALD ASSOCIATION AND ITS MINISTRIES

CHRISTIAN HERALD ASSOCIATION, founded in 1878, publishes The Christian Herald Magazine, one of the leading interdenominational religious monthlies in America. Through its wide circulation, it brings inspiring articles and the latest news of religious developments to many families. From the magazine's pages came the initiative for CHRISTIAN HERALD CHILDREN'S HOME and THE BOWERY MISSION, two individually supported not-for-profit corporations.

CHRISTIAN HERALD CHILDREN'S HOME, established in 1894, is the name for a unique and dynamic ministry to disadvantaged children, offering hope and opportunities which would not otherwise be available for reasons of poverty and neglect. The goal is to develop each child's potential and to demonstrate Christian compassion and understanding to children in need.

Mont Lawn is a permanent camp located in Bushkill, Pennsylvania. It is the focal point of a ministry which provides a healthful "vacation with a purpose" to children who without it would be confined to the streets of the city. Up to 1000 children between the ages of 7 and 11 come to Mont Lawn each year.

Christian Herald Children's Home maintains year-round contact with children by means of an *In-City Youth Ministry*. Central to its philosophy is the belief that only through sustained relationships and demonstrated concern can individual lives be truly enriched. Special emphasis is on individual guidance, spiritual and family counseling and tutoring. This follow-up ministry to inner-city children culminates for many in financial assistance toward higher education and career counseling.

THE BOWERY MISSION, located at 227 Bowery, New York City, has since 1879 been reaching out to the lost men on the Bowery, offering them what could be their last chance to rebuild their lives. Every man is fed, clothed and ministered to. Countless numbers have entered the 90-day residential rehabilitation program at the Bowery Mission. A concentrated ministry of counseling, medical care, nutrition therapy, Bible study and Gospel services awakens a man to spiritual renewal within himself.

These ministries are supported solely by the voluntary contributions of individuals and by legacies and bequests. Contributions are tax deductible. Checks should be made out either to CHRISTIAN HERALD CHILDREN'S HOME or to THE BOWERY MISSION.

Administrative Office: 40 Overlook Drive, Chappaqua, New York 10514
Telephone: (914) 769-9000